THE
PRESIDENTIAL
QUIZ BOOK

THE
PRESIDENTIAL
QUIZ BOOK

FRED L. WORTH

E PLURIBUS UNUM

BELL PUBLISHING COMPANY
New York

Dedicated to
Pamela Larm,
who brings so
much joy into my
life

This 1988 edition is published by Bell Publishing Company,
distributed by Crown Publishers, Inc.,
225 Park Avenue South, New York, New York 10003.

Printed and Bound in the United States of America

Library of Congress Cataloging-in-Publication Data

Worth, Fred L.
The presidential quiz book.

1. Presidents—United States—Miscellanea.
2. Questions and answers. I. Title.
E176.1.W94 1988   973'.09'92   87-27052
ISBN 0-517-65571-3
h g f e d c b a

CONTENTS

LIST OF PRESIDENTS ―――――――――――

A chronological list of The Presidents of the United States of America:

1. George Washington
2. John Adams
3. Thomas Jefferson
4. James Madison
5. James Monroe
6. John Quincy Adams
7. Andrew Jackson
8. Martin Van Buren
9. William Henry Harrison
10. John Tyler
11. James Knox Polk
12. Zachary Taylor
13. Millard Fillmore
14. Franklin Pierce
15. James Buchanan
16. Abraham Lincoln
17. Andrew Johnson
18. Ulysses Simpson Grant
19. Rutherford Birchard Hayes
20. James Abram Garfield

21. Chester Alan Arthur
22. (Stephen) Grover Cleveland
23. Benjamin Harrison
24. (Stephen) Grover Cleveland
25. William McKinley
26. Theodore Roosevelt
27. William Howard Taft
28. (Thomas) Woodrow Wilson
29. Warren Gamaliel Harding
30. (John) Calvin Coolidge
31. Herbert Clark Hoover
32. Franklin Delano Roosevelt
33. Harry S Truman
34. Dwight David Eisenhower
35. John Fitzgerald Kennedy
36. Lyndon Baines Johnson
37. Richard Milhous Nixon
38. Gerald Rudolph Ford
39. James Earl Carter, Jr.
40. Ronald Wilson Reagan

President of the Confederate States of America:

1. Jefferson Davis

PREFACE _____

History is comprised of people and events. This book is about the Presidents, Vice Presidents, First Ladies, and others who populate the history of the American presidency.

The Presidential Quiz Book consists of 200 quizzes containing more than 2000 fascinating questions about these all-too-human people who had their faults, frustrations, and tragic flaws just like the rest of us. Yet they also had something different—a special strength and vision that drove them to seek the highest office of political influence and power. Had these men not been elected President they surely would have made their marks in other fields.

Why did fate choose these men to serve as the heads of state of the most powerful country in the history of the world, and whom did fate prevent from holding that position? Naturally, one can only speculate on the course of history. But how these men lived and what they did *can* be questioned, and that is the purpose of this book.

To know the history of the Presidents is to know American history. And to know American history is one of the most valuable and necessary tools for the exercise of democracy.

Here's your chance to show what you do—and don't—know about the Presidents and about the history of the United States. If you have learned anything about American history from reading this book then it will have been worth the price of admission.

The Quizzes

QUIZ 1: RECORDS (INTRODUCTORY QUIZ) _____

1. Who was the first President of the United States?

2. Who is the current President of the United States?

3. Who is the first President listed alphabetically by his last name?

4. Who is the last President listed alphabetically by his last name?

5. Who was the tallest President at 6' 4"?

6. Who was the shortest President at just 5' 4"?

7. What President weighed the most at 332 pounds?

8. What President lived the longest?

9. What President died at the youngest age?

10. Who is the only President to have served two nonconsecutive terms?

If you enjoyed this first quiz, just wait until you read the last quiz in the book, Tough and Tricky Questions.

QUIZ 2: ACTORS _____

1. What President was a member of Harvard University's Hasty Pudding Club?

2. What actress, who has a star on the Hollywood Walk of Fame, opposed Richard Nixon for the U.S. Senate in 1950?

3. What English actress played the lead role in the play *Our American Cousin,* which was presented at Ford's Theatre the evening that President Abraham Lincoln was assassinated?

4. What Hollywood actor of TV westerns ran for President on the Populist Party ticket in 1984?

5. What Presidential assassin appeared as a performer in the Shakespearean play *Richard III* at Ford's Theatre?

6. How many movies did First Lady Nancy Davis Reagan appear in during her film career, which lasted from 1949 through 1958?

7. Stage actress Priscilla Cooper, who lived in the White House, was the daughter-in-law of which President?

8. What First Lady appeared in such film classics as *Becky Sharp* (1935), *The Great Ziegfeld* (1936), and *Small Town Girl* (1936)?

9. Name the Shakespearean actor who was the brother of assassin John Wilkes Booth and a member of the Hall of Fame of great Americans.

10. What former President appeared with his wife in a party scene in a December 1983 episode of the TV series "Dynasty"?

11. Impressed by the 1976 movie *Taxi Driver,* what actor was John Hinkley, Jr., trying to emulate, and which actress was he trying to impress when he attempted to shoot President Ronald Reagan?

12. What President's daughter named Lynda dated actor George Hamilton while she lived in the White House?

13. What President's daughter appeared in the 1980 TV movie *For Ladies Only?*

14. What President's wife won an Academy Award in 1948?

15. What Hollywood actor was thrown out of Stanford University when, as a prank, he threw a dummy in front of a car, and then accused the driver of running over his brother? The car's driver was Lou Hoover, the wife of President Herbert Hoover.

QUIZ 3: ADOPTIONS/STEPPARENTS _____

1. What President adopted a young Indian boy?

2. Name the two Presidents who were born orphans.

3. What President adopted his wife's nephew?

4. Who was the only President to have a stepmother during his child-hood?

5. Who were the three other Presidents to have stepmothers, but not during their childhoods?

6. What is the name of Ronald Reagan and Jane Wyman's adopted son?

7. Harriet Lane, the orphan niece who acted as the hostess of the White House, was raised by which President?

8. What two Presidents had stepfathers?

9. What President was first named after his real father and then renamed after his stepfather?

10. What First Lady lost both her mother and her father by age of ten?

QUIZ 4: ADVICE _____

Choose which President gave the following advice:

1. "Whatever you say, tell the truth."
   A. Richard M. Nixon
   B. Ronald Reagan
   C. Abraham Lincoln
   D. Grover Cleveland

2. "If you see ten troubles coming down the road, you can be sure nine will run into a ditch before they reach you, and you'll have to battle with only one of these."
   A. Calvin Coolidge
   B. Woodrow Wilson
   C. Rutherford B. Hayes
   D. Harry S Truman

3. "Be sincere, be brief, be seated."
   A. George Washington
   B. Thomas Jefferson
   C. Franklin D. Roosevelt
   D. John F. Kennedy

QUIZ 5: AGES _____

1. Who was the youngest man to become President of the United States?

2. Who was the youngest man elected President of the United States?

3. What is the minimum age for anyone to be elected President?

4. What is the minimum age for anyone to be elected Vice President?

5. Who was the oldest Vice President to become President upon the death of a President?

6. Who were the only two Presidents to live past the age of ninety?

7. At what age was Franklin Pierce elected President of the United States?

8. The engraving of Abraham Lincoln on the $5 bill captures him at what age?

9. Who was the oldest man to be elected President at the age of sixty-nine?

10. What President was married for the first time at the age of forty-three?

11. Who was the first President to reach the age of seventy while serving as President?

12. The greatest age difference between an incoming President and outgoing President was twenty-eight years. Who were these two men?

13. What President was married to the youngest First Lady, twenty-one-year-old Frances Folson?

14. What President was the last living signer of the Constitution, and the last living member of the Continental Congress?

15. What First Lady lived the longest and died at the age of ninety-seven?

16. What President married his second wife at the age of sixty-two?

17. How old was President John Tyler when he became a father for the fifteenth and last time?

18. How old was President Andrew Johnson when he became a father for the first time?

19. Who was the first President younger than his Vice President?

20. Who was the last President younger than his Vice President?

QUIZ 6: ALL IN THE FAMILY _____

1. What President married his third cousin?

2. What President married his wife's niece Mary?

3. What President married his fifth cousin once removed?

4. What two men who were father and son both served as President?

5. What two men who were grandfather and grandson both served as President?

6. Who was the brother of a President and the father of a First Lady?

7. What First Lady was also the mother of a President?

8. Who was the son of one President and the father of another President?

9. Name the President who was assassinated, and whose younger brother, later a Presidential candidate, was also assassinated.

10. What man was the grandson of one President and the son-in-law of another?

QUIZ 7: AMBASSADORS AND MINISTERS _____

1. What President served as ambassador to France, Holland, and Great Britain?

2. What President served as minister to France from 1785 to 1789?

3. What President served as the first U.S. minister to Russia, and then served as minister to the court of St. James?

4. President Grover Cleveland appointed what ex-President as ambassador to Paraguay and to Uraguay?

5. Mrs. Anne Armstrong became the first female ambassador to the Court of St. James. What President appointed her?

6. The fathers of what two Presidents both served as ambassadors to the Court of St. James?

7. The U.S. Senate rejected, by just one vote, what future President as minister to the Court of St. James in 1831?

8. What ambassador to France was angrily recalled in 1796 by President George Washington because a commitment he made to France jeopardized the neutrality of the United States?

9. What President served as ambassador to the Court of St. James as did his father and his son Charles?

10. How many Presidents have served as minister to the Court of St. James?

Extra. Who is the only President to have served as minister to Spain?

Extra. President Richard M. Nixon appointed the son of which previous President as ambassador to Belgium?

QUIZ 8: ANCESTORS _____

1. Who was the first President born of Indian ancestry?

2. What two Presidents shared the same great-grandfather?

3. Robert Morris is the common ancestor of which two Presidents?

4. Of which President was President Harry S Truman's paternal grand-mother a direct descendant through that President's brother?

5. What President claimed to have been a direct descendant of the American hero Paul Revere?

6. Geneologists have discovered that what President was related to eleven other Presidents?

7. To which American Indian princess was President Woodrow Wilson's second wife, Edith Galt, related?

8. What two Presidents were descended from Claes Maertenszen Van Rosenvelt of Holland, and how are the two related?

9. What President was the great-great-grandson of Pilgram John Alder and his wife Priscilla?

10. Actress and singer Judy Garland was the first cousin three times removed of which President?

Extra. Actress Lillian Gish claimed to be a descendant of which President?

QUIZ 9: ANIMALS _____

1. The daughter of which President kept two Jersey cows on the White House grounds to assure fresh milk and butter each day?

2. The First Lady of which President kept a Holstein cow named Pauline grazing on the White House grounds?

3. The wife of which President raised sheep on the White House lawn, which produced $100,000 for the Red Cross during the War?

4. The squirrels on the White House grounds were rounded up after they had been interfering with which President's putting practices?

5. What President owned a jackass named Royal Gift?

6. What future President once returned the missing dog of Sir William Howe, the commander in chief of the British Army?

7. The sons of which President owned a bear named Jonathan Edwards?

8. First Lady Grace Coolidge owned what sort of unusual pet named Rebecca?

9. What type of animal did Meriwether Lewis give to President Thomas Jefferson, who kept it at Monticello?

10. Theodore Roosevelt's daughter, Alice, owned what kind of pet animal named Emily Spinach?

QUIZ 10: APPOINTMENTS _____

1. What President appointed Frances Perkins as Secretary of Labor, making her the first woman to be appointed to a cabinet post?

2. Ruth Bryan Owens, daughter of William Jennings Bryan, was the first woman to be appointed minister (to Denmark). What President appointed her?

3. Who was the President who appointed William Howard Taft to the Supreme Court?

4. What was the name of the thirty-two-year-old man that George Washington selected as Secretary of the Treasury?

5. Name the Secretary of Agriculture selected by President William McKinley who would occupy that office for sixteen years.

6. What Vice President served as the Secretary of Agriculture, as had his father?

7. What President appointed Juanita M. Kreps, the first female director of the New York Stock Exchange, to serve as his Secretary of Commerce?

8. President Harry S Truman appointed Allen Varley Astin as the director of the National Bureau of Standards. Who is the actor son of Allen Astin?

9. What Attorney General appointed by Richard M. Nixon served as Lt. John F. Kennedy's commanding officer in the Solomon Islands during World War II?

10. Name the millionaire who served as Secretary of the Treasury under both Presidents Calvin Coolidge and Herbert Hoover.

QUIZ 11: ASSASSINATIONS AND ATTEMPTS _____

1. What future President served on the Warren Commission, which studied the assassination of President John F. Kennedy?

2. A house painter named Richard Lawrence pointed two pistols at the Chief Executive, but both misfired. What President was the object of this, the first attempted assassination of a President?

3. Who was the first President to be assassinated?

4. Anton Cermak, the mayor of Chicago, was killed in Miami, Florida, by Guiseppe Zangara, in an attempt on the life of which President?

5. What President had two assassination attempts against him within a period of one month?

6. Saloon keeper John F. Schrank shot and wounded what ex-President in Milwaukee, Wisconsin?

7. Who was the only President to sign the papers ordering the hanging of the man who had attempted to assassinate him?

8. Robert Todd Lincoln was present at or shortly after the assassination of which three Presidents?

9. What was the name of the District of Columbia attorney general who prosecuted Richard Lawrence for his attempted assassination of President Andrew Jackson?

10. Assassin John Wilkes Booth was born in 1839. In what year was assassin Lee Harvey Oswald born?

QUIZ 12: AUTHORS _____

1. Nobel Prize–winning author John Steinbeck sat on the rostrum of which President's inauguration?

2. What President borrowed the term "New Deal" from his favorite author's novel, *A Connecticut Yankee in King Arthur's Court?*

3. About which President did Walt Whitman write his poem, "O Captain! My Captain"?

4. Author Washington Irving was a lifelong friend of which President?

5. Mark Twain published the autobiography of which former President and made money for the ex-President but went into debt himself?

6. What President was both a friend and classmate of author Nathaniel Hawthorne at Bowdoin College? (Hawthorne dedicated one of his books to him.)

7. What book by Upton Sinclair prompted President Theodore Roosevelt to lobby for the Pure Food and Drug Act (1906)?

8. Author Richard Henry Dana, who wrote the book *Two Years Before the Mast* and later served as minister to Britain, was the cousin of which President?

9. Author Gore Vidal, who wrote historical novels such as *Burr* and *Lincoln,* was a cousin of which President?

10. Name the author who wrote the 1955 book, *The Day Lincoln Was Shot,* and in 1968 wrote *The Day Kennedy Was Shot.*

QUIZ 13: AUTOBIOGRAPHIES _____

1. What President wrote his autobiography, *An American Epic*, in long-hand?

2. *Why Not the Best?* is the title of the autobiography of which President based on a question once asked him by Admiral Hyman Rickover?

3. What President never once mentioned his wife, Hannah, in his auto-biography?

4. Who was the first President to write an autobiography?

5. What President co-authored with his wife an autobiography entitled *When All the Glory Is Gone*, after which they swore they would never write together again?

6. *Autobiography* was the story of which former First Lady? It was published in 1961, just one year before her death.

7. What former First Lady wrote two autobiographies, *The Times of My Life* (1978) and *A Glad Awakening* (1987)?

8. *The First Lady of Plains* was the 1985 autobiograpy of which former First Lady?

9. The title of Ronald Reagan's 1965 autobiography was based on a line that he spoke in the 1941 movie *King's Row*. Name the book.

10. Name the President whose autobiography bears the same title as his initials.

QUIZ 14: AUTOMOBILES _____

1. Who was the only President to drive an electric automobile?

2. The first President to ride in an automobile did so in Hartford, Connecticut, in a Columbia Electric Victoria. Who was he?

3. What was the first automobile owned by Jimmy and Rosalynn Carter after their marriage?

4. What President liked to ride in the Presidential convertible nicknamed the Sunshine Special?

5. What President rode in a Presidential limousine that had an extra-high roof to accommodate top hats?

6. Who was the first President to ride in a bubbletop automobile?

7. Who was the last President to ride to his inauguration in a horse-drawn carriage?

8. What is the only currently manufactured automobile named for a U.S. President?

9. Who was serving as President when the White House received its first fleet of three automobiles?

10. The son of which President was once the leading distributor of the Fiat automobiles in the United States?

Extra. Who became the first President to ride in an armor-plated Presidential automobile?

QUIZ 15: AVIATION _____

1. During which President's administration did the first successful balloon flight in the United States take place?

2. Who was the only President sworn into office on board an airplane?

3. Only one President owned a pilot's license. Name him.

4. Who was the first President to fly in an airplane?

5. What was the name of the Kennedy family airplane—a converted Convair?

6. What President was awarded the Silver Star during World War II for having been a passenger on board a B-26 hit by Japanese bullets?

7. What President lost money investing in an intercity dirigible freight line?

8. Who was the first President to fly in a helicopter while in office?

9. What is the tactical call sign of an Air Force DC-3 if the President is on board?

10. What is the tactical call sign of a Marine Corps helicopter when the President is on board?

QUIZ 16: AWARDS _____

1. What President won a Pulitzer Prize for writing the book *Profiles In Courage?*

2. What President won a Nobel Peace Prize in 1919?

3. What President won a Nobel Peace Prize for settling the Russo-Japanese War in 1905?

4. Name the President who was named MVP (Most Valuable Player) as a center for the University of Michigan's football team.

5. What President received a gold medal from the Agricultural Society of Paris for inventing a new plow?

6. What President was nominated for the Congressional Medal of Honor for his bravery during the Spanish-American War?

7. What President as a general became the first foreigner to win Russia's Order of Victory?

8. What President received the Purple Heart, the Navy Cross, and the Marine Corps medal?

9. Congress planned to award what President the Congressional Medal of Honor on his eighty-seventh birthday, but he turned it down?

10. What Vice President won the Nobel Peace Prize in 1925 for creating a plan to stabilize the German economy after World War I?

11. What President received the country's highest medal (at the time) while he was serving as a soldier?

12. Who was the first President to award the Purple Heart, originally called the Badge of Military Merit, which bears his likeness?

13. Who was the first President to present the Congressional Medal of Honor?

14. Who was the only First Lady ever to win a special Emmy Award?

15. What President was once nominated for a Grammy Award?

QUIZ 17: BATTLES _____

1. What President won a battle that was fought two weeks after the War of 1812 had ended?

2. What President was thrown from his horse and injured in the groin during his only battle in the Mexican War?

3. Leading Battery D of the 129th Field Artillery, Harry S Truman saw combat during which war?

4. What President was wounded in the left arm during the Battle of Antietam during the Civil War?

5. What President defeated General Santa Anna's larger army of 20,000 at Buena Vista with only 5000 volunteers?

6. What President fainted twice during the heat of battle in the Mexican War?

7. What President lead a group of volunteer soldiers up Cuba's San Juan Hill?

8. In 1864 President Abraham Lincoln was present at what fort where he viewed his only Civil War battle?

9. What President and First Lady were living in China during the Boxer Rebellion when a shell hit their house?

10. Which President had a son who, at less than thirteen years of age, followed his father, a general at the time, into battle and was wounded at Vicksburg?

QUIZ 18: BIOGRAPHIES ⸻⸻

1. What former President wrote *The Ordeal of Woodrow Wilson* in 1958?

2. George Washington was the subject of a biography written by which President?

3. Who is the most written about President of the United States with over forty biographies?

4. The son (Charles Phelps) of which President authored the 1936 biography *You and I and Roosevelt?*

5. With which President did John R. Stiles write *Portrait of an Assassin*, a biography of Lee Harvey Oswald?

6. What poet and historian won a Pulitzer Prize for his biographical series on President Abraham Lincoln?

7. The daughter (Julie) of which President wrote the 1977 book *Special People* about the lives of six people she had met?

8. The daughter of which President wrote the 1976 book *Women of Courage*, which presented twelve profiles of women in American history?

9. What President wrote an 1887 biography of Senator Thomas Hart Benton?

10. *The Life of George Washington* was a biography written by which President?

QUIZ 19: BIRDS _____

1. President Calvin Coolidge's family had two pet birds named Nip and Tuck. What kind of birds were they?

2. What First Lady owned a green parrot?

3. The popular song "Listen to the Mockingbird" was dedicated by its composer to the niece of which President?

4. What President owned a pet mockingbird named Bill that liked to sit on its master's shoulder?

5. What was the name of President Andrew Jackson's pet parrot that attended his master's funeral?

6. What President as a young boy shot and killed a wild turkey, an act that upset him so deeply that he never used a gun again?

7. What President owned a pet parrot that could whistle a few lines of "Yankee Doodle"?

8. What President and First Lady appeared together in a television play entitled "A Turkey for the President"?

9. The son (Tad) of which President owned a pet turkey named Jack?

10. What bird did founding father Benjamin Franklin want to make the national symbol of the United States instead of the eagle?

QUIZ 20: BIRTHPLACES _____

1. Who was the first President born in a log cabin?

2. Who was the first President born west of the Mississippi River?

3. How many Presidents have been born in the state of Virginia?

4. Tampico, Illinois, a town of 1200, was, on February 6, 1911, the birthplace of which President?

5. Both North and South Carolina claim the birthplace of which President?

6. Who was the first President born beyond the boundaries of the original thirteen states?

7. This President's New York City birthplace is now a museum located at 28 East 20th Street.

8. Name the two Presidents who were not only born in the same town but also on the same street.

9. What President's birthplace in Denison, Texas, is under the supervision of the Texas Department of Parks and Wildlife?

10. What President was born in a town named for his grandfather?

11. What President's birthplace was preserved by the United Auto Workers, who then presented it to the state of Missouri as a historical site?

12. What President's birthplace is now on display on the campus of Mercerburg Academy?

13. What state is the birthplace of eight Vice Presidents?

14. What President and his Vice President were both born in Charles City County, Virginia?

15. What three consecutive Presidents were all born in Ohio?

QUIZ 21: BIRTHS _____

1. Who was the first President born on the Fourth of July?

2. Who was the first President born in the twentieth century?

3. Who was the first President born on the West Coast?

4. In 1924 who was the first President born in a hospital?

5. On December 5, 1782, who was the first President to be born a citizen of the United States and not a British subject?

6. Warren G. Harding was the last of seven Presidents to be born in which state?

7. More Presidents were born during what month of the year than any other?

8. What is the only month in which no President has ever been born?

9. What President was actually born in Fairfield, Vermont, on October 5, 1829, although he claimed to have been born in 1830?

10. What President was born in 1856, the same year in which James Buchanan was elected President?

Extra. What President was born February 12, 1809, on the same day as naturalist Charles Darwin?

QUIZ 22: BOATS AND SHIPS _____

1. Who was the first President to travel on a steamship (the *Savannah*)?

2. What President was the engineering officer on board the nuclear submarine *Sea Wolf?*

3. What was the number of Lt. John F. Kennedy's PT-boat that was rammed and sunk during World War II?

4. What President served on an aircraft carrier during World War II?

5. Name the President whose brother served on board a U.S. Navy destroyer named after their oldest brother.

6. On what ship named for a President did President Woodrow Wilson travel to France to attend the Paris Peace Conference?

7. Theodore Roosevelt won the Nobel Prize after the Russo-Japanese agreement was signed in 1905 on board what Presidential yacht?

8. The sinking of what ship was referred to by President Theodore Roosevelt as "murder on the high seas"?

9. What was the name of the last Presidential yacht, which President Jimmy Carter auctioned off in 1977?

10. What President sent the Great White Fleet of sixteen battleships on a cruise around the world to show American strength?

QUIZ 23: BOOKS _____

1. What President wrote thirty-seven books with titles such as *The New Nationalism* and *African Game Trails?*

2. Who is the only President to have had a book of poetry published (in 1832)?

3. Congress authorized the purchase of whose personal library as the basis of the new Library of Congress?

4. In 1909 what engineer and President authored the book *Principles of Mining?*

5. What President wrote articles for the *Ladies Home Journal* after which they were sold in book form?

6. What President's father wrote a book in 1936 entitled *I'm For Roosevelt?*

7. What book, written by John F. Kennedy as his undergraduate thesis at Harvard, featured an introduction by Henry Luce?

8. What Vice President and historian wrote the ten-volume series *A History of the United States from 1834 to 1874?*

9. In 1906 the book *Fishing and Shooting Sketches* was published. What President was the author?

10. Henry Cabot Lodge collaborated with which President in 1895 to write *Hero Tales from American History?*

11. What two books by Presidents have been made into television series?

12. *To Love a Child* was the title of a 1982 book written by which First Lady?

13. What child of a President authored the 1984 novel *Murder and the First Lady* in which his mother was the subject?

14. What President wrote the 1979 book *A Time for Healing?*

15. What author wrote a narrative history of American politics in the series, *The Making of the President?*

QUIZ 24: BOYHOOD _____

1. What President was the spelling champion of Massachusetts at the age of ten in 1745?

2. What President as a boy drove barge teams along the Ohio and Erie canals?

3. What President developed blood poisoning in one of his legs and when told by his doctor that it would have to be amputated, refused?

4. As a child what President was taken on a visit to the White House where President Grover Cleveland said to him, "My little man, I am going to make a strange wish for you, may you never be President of the United States"?

5. What President when he reached the age of twenty-one received a one million dollar trust fund that had been set up by his father?

QUIZ 25: BREAKING THE LAW _____

1. What President was once asked to resign his command by his commanding officer or face a court-martial because he was drunk?

2. What President was expelled from Dickinson College in Carlisle, Pennsylvania, for disorderly conduct?

3. What President saw the most cabinet members investigated for wrongdoing?

4. What President was arrested in 1853 for accidently running down a woman while he was on horseback? (When it was discovered whom he was, the police officer let him go.)

5. What President ran away from his indentured servitude as a young boy in Raleigh, North Carolina? (There was a $10 reward for his return.)

6. Washington, D.C. police officer William West once arrested what President for speeding his horse and buggy down M street?

7. What President married his wife, Rachel, before she was legally divorced from her first husband?

8. Who was the first person sentenced to life imprisonment for an attempted assassination on the life of a President?

9. Name President Warren G. Harding's Secretary of the Interior who became the first cabinet member convicted of a crime (bribery).

10. What President along with his brother Joseph once spent a night in jail as a teenager?

QUIZ 26: BROKEN PROMISES _____

1. What President ran against Wendell Willkie with the promise to voters that American troops would not be sent to "any foreign war"?

2. On two occasions what President put in writing his promise to quit politics, but didn't?

3. What President not only broke his promise to support the one federal union to endorse him for President, but also broke that union?

4. What President won the election partly because of his 1916 campaign slogan "He kept us out of war" and then declared war on Germany?

5. What President vowed that there would not, under any condition, be an intervention in Cuba by U.S. troops only five days before Cuba was invaded?

QUIZ 27: BROTHERS _____

1. The brother of which President served as Attorney General?

2. Sam Houston was the name of the brother of which Texas-born President?

3. Which President's brother was the anchorman of his high school graduating class of twenty-six students?

4. What President had a twin brother and sister named Randolph and Ann?

5. What President's brother received a secret $200,000 loan from billionaire Howard Hughes?

6. What President's brother was given a loan by Libyan ruler Muammar al-Qaddafi?

7. The brother (Milton) of which President served as the president of three American universities: Kansas State, Penn State, and Johns Hopkins?

8. President Howard Taft's half-brother Charles F. Taft was the owner of which major league baseball team?

9. What two Presidents were both the brothers of clergymen?

10. What two Presidents had brothers who were generals in the U.S. Army?

11. Who was the only President to have two brothers serve in the U.S. Senate?

12. The brother (David) of which President served as the U.S. consul general to Hawaii?

13. Two brothers of which President died on board the same ship?

14. Which one of John F. Kennedy's brothers did Joseph Kennedy, Sr., originally plan to groom to become President?

QUIZ 28: BURIALS _____

1. Who was the only President buried in Washington, D.C., with his final resting place in the Washington Cathedral?

2. What President was buried near his boyhood friend, Dabney Carr, with whom he made a pact to be interred under the same oak tree?

3. What President was buried the farthest south?

4. What evangelist officiated at the burial of Lyndon B. Johnson in 1973?

5. What President was buried in a Kentucky National Cemetery named for him?

6. In what state are the most Vice Presidents buried?

7. Who was the only Vice President buried in Washington, D.C.?

8. Although eight Vice Presidents were born in New York and nine Vice Presidents died in New York, who was the only Vice President buried in New York City?

9. What West German cemetery did President Ronald Reagan visit on May 5, 1985, in which members of the Gestapo were buried?

10. In what city were three Vice Presidents buried in the Crown Hill Cemetery?

Extra. The wife of which President was the only First Lady buried at Arlington National Cemetery?

Extra. What President was buried under a willow tree that had its roots taken from that of a willow at Napoleon's gravesite on Saint Helena Island?

QUIZ 29: BUSINESS _____

1. The Union Carbide Corporation was founded from a small business started by the son of which President?

2. What President uttered the famous words: "The business of America is business"?

3. Which brother of President Richard M. Nixon founded a chain of California restaurants in 1956 that sold Nixonburgers?

4. During which President's administration was the Federal Trade Commission established to regulate business?

5. The father of which President founded Somerset Importers in order to stockpile cases of liquor while waiting for the end of Prohibition?

QUIZ 30: THE CABINET _____

1. What President appointed Oscar S. Straus as Secretary of the Department of Commerce and Labor, making him the first Jewish cabinet member?

2. What President was the only Chief Executive to maintain his cabinet intact for an entire administration?

3. The son of which President once served as President James Garfield's Secretary of War?

4. Franklin D. Roosevelt, Jr., served as Undersecretary of Commerce under which two Presidents?

5. James R. Garfield, the son of former President James Garfield, served as the Secretary of the Interior under which President?

6. Robert Weaver, the first Secretary of the Department of Housing and Urban Development, became the first black to hold a cabinet post. What President appointed him in January, 1966?

7. The son of which President served as Undersecretary of State in President Dwight D. Eisenhower's cabinet?

8. Who became the first cabinet member, other than Secretary of State, to become President?

9. Who was the only President to hold two cabinet posts?

10. What President had a Vice President named John Calhoun, a Secretary of War named John Eaton, an Attorney General named John Berrien, a Postmaster General named John McLean, and a Secretary of the Navy named John Branch?

11. Charles Lee, President George Washington's Attorney General, was the brother of which soldier?

12. Who was the only President whose daughter married a member of his cabinet?

13. What President made a record twenty-six changes to his cabinet, all within a four-year period?

14. Who was the only President to serve as Secretary of Commerce in two cabinets, Warren G. Harding's and Calvin Coolidge's?

15. What President appointed a man with the middle name of Strange to serve as Secretary of Defense?

Extra. What President's cabinet was said to have consisted of millionaires and one plumber?

QUIZ 31: CABINET NICKNAMES _____

Match the President with his cabinet's nickname:

1. Poker Cabinet

2. Tennis Cabinet

3. Medicine Ball Cabinet

4. Kitchen Cabinet

5. The Brain Trust

A. Andrew Jackson

B. Herbert Hoover

C. Franklin D. Roosevelt

D. Warren G. Harding

E. Theodore Roosevelt

QUIZ 32: CAMPAIGN SLOGANS _____

1. What President was re-elected with the slogan "He kept us out of war"?

2. "A return to normalcy" was the promise of which candidate for the Presidency?

3. "Prosperity is just around the corner" was the optimistic campaign promise of which President?

4. What losing candidate used the slogan "In your heart you know he's right"?

5. In Albuquerque, New Mexico, an unknown man in the audience yelled out what unofficial slogan to Harry S Truman?

6. "All the way with _____" was the campaign slogan of which Presidential candidate?

7. "Keep cool with _____" was the campaign slogan of which Presidential candidate?

8. Finish this colorful campaign slogan by the Democrats: "We Polked you in 1844, we shall _____ you in 1852."

9. What First Lady began the "Keep American Beautiful" campaign, which included the removal of many highway billboards?

10. What did the initials WIN mean in President Gerald Ford's WIN Campaign?

QUIZ 33: CAMPAIGN SONGS ————————

1. What song by Jack Yellen and Milton Ager served as Franklin D. Roosevelt's 1932 Presidential campaign song?

2. The Academy Award–winning song "High Hopes" was the campaign song of which candidate?

3. What popular entertainer composed Warren G. Harding's campaign song "Harding, You're the Man for Us"?

4. What popular composer wrote the 1952 campaign song "I Like Ike" for Dwight D. Eisenhower?

QUIZ 34: CANDIDATES _____

1. Nominated in 1872 by the National Women's Suffrage Association, who was the first woman to run for the Presidency?

2. What Socialist candidate received 920,000 votes for the Presidency while in jail in 1920?

3. What Union general turned down a bid for the Presidency, stating: "If nominated, I will not accept. If elected, I will not serve"?

4. What President became the first dark horse candidate when he was nominated on the eighth ballot at the Democratic Convention?

5. What candidate, who made famous the saying "Go West, young man, go West," was nominated for the Presidency in 1872?

6. Norman Thomas ran for President in every election from 1928 to 1948 on what ticket?

7. Name the feminist and lawyer who was the first woman to plead a case before the U.S. Supreme Court, and who ran for President in 1884 and 1888 on the National Equal Rights Party ticket.

8. What Presidential candidate ran for the Presidency three times, but lost the second and third times?

9. What circus clown, who was the model for the painting of Uncle Sam, sought the Republican nomination for President in 1868?

10. Who was the first black to run for the Vice Presidency?

QUIZ 35: CHILDREN _____

1. Married twice, what President fathered fifteen children, the last when he was seventy years old?

2. What President's son (George Washington) was born in Berlin, Germany, and daughter (Louisa Catherine) was born in St. Petersburg, Russia?

3. Who was the only President to name two of his sons after former Presidents?

4. What President had the only child (William) to die in the White House?

5. The son of which President died in 1924 of a blister on his toe from playing in a game of lawn tennis?

Extra. What two Presidents became fathers while serving as President?

QUIZ 36: THE CIVIL WAR _____

1. What former President of the United States served as a member of the Confederate Congress from 1861 to 1862?

2. What President's son (Richard) served as a brigadier general during the Civil War?

3. What Union general ran against President Abraham Lincoln for the Presidency in 1864?

4. Both the loser, James G. Blaine, and the winner of the 1884 Presidential election hired substitutes for themselves during the Civil War. Name the President.

5. What President was the field commander of the Union army during the Civil War?

6. The wife of which President was accused of spying for the Confederacy during the Civil War?

7. The son of which President served as the United States minister to Great Britain during the Civil War?

8. What President was a mess sergeant nicknamed Sergeant Billie during the Civil War?

9. What President was Sergeant Billie's commanding officer?

10. What President was the only senator from a seceding state (Tennessee) to remain in the Senate, ignoring demands from his state to resign?

11. What Vice President served as a Confederate major general and Confederate Secretary of State during the Civil War?

12. Who was first offered but turned down the Presidency of the Confederacy?

13. How many Presidents served in the military during the Civil War?

14. Who was the only President to serve in both the Mexican War and the Civil War?

15. The Confederate States of America were organized during the administration of which President?

QUIZ 37: CLOSE FRIENDS AND ADVISORS _____

Match the President with his friend or advisor:

1. Dave Powers   A. John F. Kennedy

2. Bebe Rebozo   B. Woodrow Wilson

3. Louis Howe   C. Richard M. Nixon

4. Colonel Edward M. House   D. Franklin D. Roosevelt

5. Edwin Meese   E. Ronald Reagan

QUIZ 38: COINCIDENCES _____

1. In April 1951 while President Harry S Truman was throwing out the opening day baseball at Griffin Park in Washington, D.C., what man, whom he had fired, was being given a ticker tape parade in New York City?

2. What Vice President under President Franklin D. Roosevelt replaced a Vice President who had the same last name as his wife's maiden name?

3. Japan's surrender on September 2, 1945, which ended World War II, took place on what U.S. battleship named for President Harry S Truman's home state?

4. What notorious gangster was present at Griffin Stadium on the day that President Herbert Hoover threw out the opening day baseball?

5. What two Presidents both graduated from Harvard, attended Columbia University Law School, ran for the Vice Presidency, served as governors of New York, and were Assistant Secretaries of the Navy?

6. On June 6, 1944 (D-Day), while General Dwight D. Eisenhower was commanding the forces in Europe, what was his son John doing?

7. Every assassinated President's surname has had how many letters?

8. All bearded Presidents have all belonged to what political party?

9. What former First Lady died in October 1961, the same day she was to dedicate a new bridge over the Potomac River named after her late husband and commemorating his birthday?

10. What President had six letters in his first, middle, and last names, 666, the same number as the Antichrist?

11. As a little girl, she danced with a group named the Dancing Lollipops at the White House for Vice President Richard M. Nixon; as an adult, she tried to assassinate the President. Name her.

12. Possibly the most remarkable coincidence in American history occurred when which two signers of the Declaration of Independence died on the same day, the fiftieth anniversary of the signing of the document?

13. What President died on November 22, the anniversary of the death of his paternal great-grandfather, who also died shortly after the birth of a son (Patrick)?

14. What has happened to every President since 1840 who was elected in a year ending with a zero?

15. Presidents Abraham Lincoln, William Henry Harrison, William McKinley, and Franklin D. Roosevelt have all died in office. What was their common astrological sign?

QUIZ 39: COLLEGES _____

1. What Charlottesville educational facility founded by Thomas Jefferson opened in 1819?

2. What President served as the president of Princeton University?

3. How many colleges have been named after President George Washington?

4. Presidents James Monroe, Thomas Jefferson, and John Tyler all graduated from what Virginia college?

5. Who was the first West Point graduate elected President?

6. What President served as president of Columbia University?

7. What President earned a Ph.D. from Johns Hopkins University?

8. Seventeen-year-old Woodrow Wilson enrolled at the College of New Jersey. What is the name of that college today?

9. What President graduated first in his class at the University of North Carolina in Chapel Hill?

10. What President graduated from Harvard University at the top of his class?

11. Who was the only President in the twentieth century not to attend college?

12. What President was a member of Stanford University's first graduating class?

13. Name the five Presidents who attended Harvard University.

14. On April 13, 1776, what institution of higher learning became the first college to confer an honorary degree upon a President?

15. What President was a co-founder of Vincennes University?

QUIZ 40: COMMITTEES _____

1. What President was a member of the Warren Commission that studied the assassination of President John F. Kennedy?

2. What President was a member of the House Un-American Activities Committee in the early 1950s?

3. What President testified in front of the House Un-American Activities Committee in the early 1950s?

4. What three Presidents served on the University of Virginia's Board of Visitors (the governing board)?

5. Who was the first Vice President to sit on the National Security Council?

Extra. Name the only President who appeared before the Committee on the Conduct of the War to defend his wife.

QUIZ 41: CONGRESS _____

1. What President spent a record seventeen years in Congress prior to being elected President?

2. Who was the only son of a President to serve in both the Senate and the House of Representatives?

3. Who was the first President to make an appearance before Congress (April 8, 1913)?

4. Who served as Congressman from Massachusetts for eighteen years following his term as President?

5. What President did the House of Representatives unsuccessfully attempt to impeach?

Extra. What President did Congress successfully impeach but failed by one vote to convict?

Extra. Name the only two Presidents who did not deliver a State of the Union message to Congress.

QUIZ 42: CUSTOMS _____

1. What President introduced the custom of shaking hands (rather than bowing) at official receptions?

2. The President of the United States is honored with a _____-gun salute.

3. Former Presidents of the United States are honored with a _____-gun salute.

4. What President issued a proclamation that called for the last Thursday in November to be observed as Thanksgiving Day?

5. What President began the custom of refusing renomination for a third term of office so that the country could have a new leader?

QUIZ 43: DATES AND YEARS _____

1. Name the only two Presidents born on the same day of the year, November 2.

2. On what date is the Presidential inauguration held every four years?

3. On what date is the national election held every four years?

4. Prior to the passage of the Twentieth Amendment that set inauguration day on January 20, on what date were Presidential inaugurations held?

5. In what year did the Nineteenth Amendment give women the right to vote in the national election?

6. Name the three Presidents of the United States during the year 1841.

7. What two Presidents both died in 1826?

8. What two Presidents died in 1901?

9. For how many years must a candidate for the Presidency have resided in the United States?

10. Both the wife and the mother of which President died on the same day, February 14, 1884?

QUIZ 44: DAUGHTERS _____

1. What President once said of his daughter Alice, "I can do one of two things, I can be President of the United States or I can control Alice, I cannot do both"?

2. The daughter (Eliza) of which President married George Hay, who prosecuted Aaron Burr for treason?

3. What President's daughter married a man who in 1981 was elected as the governor of Virginia?

4. What was the name of the first daughter born to a President?

5. The daughter (Mary Scott) of which President was younger than four of her father's grandchildren?

6. What President's daughter was listed as co-writer on the Eagles' recording of "I Wish You Love"?

7. What President fathered the first daughter born in the White House?

8. The daughter (Alice) of which President married the Speaker of the House, Nicholas Longworth?

9. The Baby Ruth candy bar, introduced in 1921 by the Curtiss Candy Company, was named after the daughter of which President (and not after baseball great Babe Ruth)?

10. The daughter (Margaret) of which President made her singing debut with the Chicago Symphony Orchestra?

QUIZ 45: DEATHS _____

1. Napoleon Bonaparte ordered ten days of mourning throughout France upon the death of which American President?

2. What President died in a house located at 135 Adams Street in Quincy, Massachusetts?

3. Who was the first President to die in office?

4. What President died (at the age of eighty) in the Speaker's Room of the House of Representatives?

5. Who was the youngest President (at forty-six) to die in office?

6. How many Presidents have died in office?

7. How many Vice Presidents have died in office?

8. What President died in the arms of a Medal of Honor winner?

9. Eight Presidents died during their terms of office. What three First Ladies died while their husbands were President?

10. What President died on December 28, 1972, followed twenty-six days later by what other President?

QUIZ 46: DEBATES _____

1. At 6'4" Abraham Lincoln was a foot taller than the man whom he debated in public on seven occasions, thus establishing his reputation. Name this man.

2. What two men were involved in what has become known as the "kitchen debate"?

3. What President headed his school's debating team at South Texas State Teacher's College?

4. What President's favorite subject in college was debating?

5. Whose debates were the subject of a four-cent U.S. postage stamp in 1958?

QUIZ 47: DEBTS _____

1. What First Lady ran up a debt of $27,000 for new clothing without informing her husband?

2. Under what President did the United States first run up a trillion-dollar debt?

3. What President owed his stockbroker nearly $200,000 at the time of his death in 1923?

4. What entertainer loaned Vice President Spiro T. Agnew $230,000 shortly after Agnew's resignation?

5. Who was President during the only time that the United States did not have a national debt?

6. What President borrowed money in order to travel to his inauguration?

7. What President as governor of New York introduced a bill abolishing prison terms for debts?

8. During what President's administration did the United States go from a creditor nation to a debtor nation owing more money than any other country in the history of the world?

9. During what President's administration was the Marshall plan put into effect to help Europe rebuild industries destroyed during World War II?

10. What President went into debt after leaving the White House when his blind trust failed to produce a profit?

QUIZ 48: DEDICATIONS _____

1. What President dedicated the Statue of Liberty in New York Harbor in 1886?

2. What airport previously named Idlewild was renamed for and dedicated to the memory of a President?

3. What President dedicated the Washington Monument?

4. On June 14, 1922, President Warren G. Harding became the first President to speak over the radio at the dedication of what memorial?

5. What President on October 13, 1932, laid the cornerstone of the new Supreme Court building in Washington?

Extra. What President dedicated the Will Rogers Memorial in Claremore, Oklahoma?

QUIZ 49: DESCENDANTS _____

1. What popular movie singer and actor (1901–1967) was a descendant of President Martin Van Buren?

2. Black editor Monroe Trotter claimed that he was a direct descendant of which American President?

3. What President had the most grandchildren (48) and the most great-grandchildren (106)?

4. Singer Grace Slick of Jefferson Starship is a descendant of which Vice President?

5. What popular actress claimed to be descended on her mother's side from President James Monroe?

QUIZ 50: DOCUMENTS _____

1. Who were the two Presidents to sign the Constitution?

2. What name was given to the principle of foreign policy adopted in 1823 that warned European nations to keep their hands off the Americas?

3. Who were the two Presidents to sign the Declaration of Independence?

4. When Thomas Jefferson completed the Declaration of Independence, what strongly worded passage did Congress delete?

5. What President co-wrote the Federalist Papers with Alexander Hamilton and John Jay?

Extra. According to legend, what document did Abraham Lincoln write on an envelope in a railroad car?

Extra. What President wrote the Massachusetts Bill of Rights, which became the model copied by other states?

QUIZ 51: DOGS _____

1. To which President did the Marquis de Lafayette send seven fox-hounds from France?

2. Charles Fred Bush was the pet cocker spaniel of which Vice President?

3. What pet dogs of which two Presidents were both the subjects of speeches?

4. What Presidential dog was originally named Big Boy?

5. What was the name of the Airedale puppy sent to President Warren G. Harding by Marshall Sheppey of Toledo, Ohio?

6. What First Lady's pet German shepherd once bit the Canadian Prime Minister?

7. What President's daughter (Maria) owned the first dog to live in the White House?

8. What was the name of the puppy that the March of Dimes poster girl presented to President Ronald Reagan and First Lady Nancy Reagan in December 1984?

9. What was the name of President Gerald Ford's golden retriever that gave birth to nine puppies in the White House kennel?

10. What were the names of President Lyndon B. Johnson's two pet beagles that were issued Washington, D.C., dog licenses #1 and #2?

QUIZ 52: ELECTIONS ─────────────

1. Who was the only man unanimously elected President in the electoral college?

2. Who was the only President elected with only one dissenting ballot in the electoral college?

3. Who did John Adams defeat in 1796 for the Presidency by just three electoral votes?

4. Who won the Presidency with fewer popular votes than Samuel Tilden, but with more electoral votes?

5. Who was the only President to win the Presidential election over a candidate who had previously beaten him for the Presidency?

6. Who was the first President elected from the Old South after the Civil War?

7. Who was the first President to receive fewer popular votes as well as fewer electoral votes than his opponent?

8. Who was the only President never to have voted in a Presidential election?

9. Who became the first President to win in the electoral college by just one vote (185 to 184)?

10. In the 1820 election, James Monroe received 231 electoral votes. How many did John Quincy Adams receive?

11. In 1848 what President won the first nationally held election?

12. Name the only two Presidential candidates who won forty-nine states in an election.

13. Who was the only President elected in an odd-numbered year?

14. William C. Clairborne's one vote in the electoral college elected Thomas Jefferson President over which opponent?

15. What President beat Coke Stevens for the Senate by just eighty-seven votes out of the 900,000 cast?

16. When Benjamin Harrison was elected as the twenty-third President in 1888, what opponent actually won more popular votes (5,540,390 to 5,444,337)?

17. When George Washington was elected as the first President in 1789, how many states cast electoral votes?

18. When President John Quincy Adams was elected with fewer electoral votes and fewer popular votes, what candidate had originally beat him in both categories?

QUIZ 53: ESTATES _____

1. What President once lived on an estate originally called Little Hunting Creek Farm?

2. What Presidential estate means "little mountain" in Italian?

3. What President called his home the Hermitage (located near Nashville, Tennessee)?

4. Who called Hyde Park, New York, his home?

5. What President's "Western White House" was located on San Clemente Island off the coast of California?

6. On January 6, 1919, what President passed away in his home at Sagamore Hill in Oyster Bay, New York?

7. Who retired in 1861 to his home, Wheatland, in Pennsylvania, after having served as President?

8. What President retired to his New York estate of Lindenwald, where he died in 1862 at the age of seventy-nine?

9. What President's Virginia estate of Oak Hills was designed by Thomas Jefferson and by architect James Hogan, the man who designed the White House?

10. What former President called his Virginia estate Sherwood Forest?

11. Andrew Jackson's estate, the Hermitage, was inspired by what other Presidential estate?

12. What President's estate was once known as Espewasson?

13. Spiegel Grove in Fremont, Ohio, was the home of which soldier and President?

14. What was the former name of Monticello, President Thomas Jefferson's estate? (It had the same name as the estate of another President.)

15. What was the name of the 688-acre California ranch purchased by Ronald Reagan in November 1974?

QUIZ 54: FASHION _____

1. The British ambassador once became indignant when which President received him wearing a pair of old carpet slippers?

2. During World War II what fashionable uniform jacket was designed for a general who would later be elected President?

3. What President had new uniforms made for the White House guards that became the butt of many jokes?

4. What company designed Lt. Col. Theodore Roosevelt's Rough Rider uniforms?

5. Who was the last President to wear knee breeches throughout his Presidency?

6. What President wore old farm clothes as a general during the Mexican War? (It was this sloppy dress that earned him the nickname of "Old Rough and Ready.")

7. What President always wore black while residing in Washington, D.C.?

8. Who was the first President inaugurated in a business suit?

9. At his 1809 inauguration, what President's attire was manufactured entirely in America?

10. What First Lady hosted the first White House fashion show for the wives of forty-three governors?

Extra. What First Lady at one time was a fashion model as well as a professional dancer?

QUIZ 55: FATHERS _____

1. Only one President was the son of a doctor. Name him.

2. Name the two Presidents who were born after the deaths of their fathers.

3. The father of which President served twice as governor of New Hampshire?

4. Who was the only President sworn into office by his father, a notary public?

5. The father of which President was once the youngest bank president in the United States at the age of twenty-five?

6. The father of which President was nicknamed "Peanuts"?

7. Name the two Presidents whose fathers signed the Declaration of Independence.

8. How many fathers of Presidents were clergymen?

9. Who was the only President whose father had been a cabinet member?

10. What was the occupation of the fathers of these First Ladies: Abigail Adams, Abigail Fillmore, Caroline Harrison, Ellen Wilson, and Jane Pierce?

11. Who was the first President whose father was alive when he was elected?

12. The father of which President was a Baptist clergyman?

13. Who were the only two Presidents to be survived by their fathers?

14. The father (David W. Wallace) of which First Lady committed suicide in 1903?

15. John Tyler, the father of President John Tyler, was the roommate of which President at the College of William and Mary?

Extra. The father of which President served as ambassador to Austria-Hungry as well as serving as Secretary of State under President Ulysses S. Grant?

Extra. The fathers of which two Presidents served as governors of Virginia?

QUIZ 56: FEDERAL EMPLOYEES _____

1. What President was said to have introduced the "spoils system"?

2. Under which President was the Civil Service Commission established in 1883?

3. What President reduced the work day for federal workers from ten hours to eight hours?

4. What President introduced the Civil Works Administration and employed four million Americans on federal, state, and local projects?

5. What President broke the federal employees union PATCO, which went on strike in 1981 to protest working conditions?

Extra. What President was given a seat on the United States Civil Service Commission in 1889 by President Benjamin Harrison?

Extra. What President issued an executive order prohibiting all federal civil servants from taking part in the running of any political organization?

Extra. What President gave thirteen of his relatives federal jobs?

QUIZ 57: FIRST LADIES _____

1. What First Lady served as the president of the American Girl Scouts?

2. Only two First Ladies remarried after the deaths of their President husbands. Grover Cleveland's wife Frances was the first; who was the second?

3. Who was the only foreign born First Lady (born in London, England, in 1775)?

4. What President married Betty Bloomer?

5. What First Lady became in 1898 the first woman graduate of geology in the United States?

6. What First Lady informed the Vice President that her husband had died and that he now was the President?

7. One First Lady was only a First Lady elect: she died before her husband took office. Who was she?

8. What popular First Lady was addicted to snuff?

9. Who was the first First Lady to die while her husband was serving as President?

10. What First Lady was known by the Secret Service as "Pinafore"?

QUIZ 58: FIRST LADIES: NICKNAMES AND TITLES _____

1. What First Lady liked to have the White House servants call her "your majesty"?
   A. Jacqueline Kennedy
   B. Dolley Madison
   C. Bess Truman
   D. Elizabeth Monroe

2. The critics of which First Lady called her "Mrs. President" because she was accused of running her huband's affairs?
   A. Abigail Adams
   B. Dolley Madison
   C. Jacqueline Kennedy
   D. Betty Ford

3. "First Lady of the World" was a nickname often conferred upon which First Lady?
   A. Nancy Davis Reagan
   B. Edith Wilson
   C. Eleanor Roosevelt
   D. Jacqueline Kennedy

4. What President addressed his wife as "Boss"?
   A. Harry S Truman
   B. Grover Cleveland
   C. Jimmy Carter
   D. Ronald Reagan

5. What affectionate nickname did President Grover Cleveland call his young wife, Frances?
   A. Bobbie
   B. Frankie
   C. Franny
   D. Tiger

QUIZ 59: FIRST LADIES: PORTRAYALS —

1. What First Lady was portrayed by Shelley Duvall in the 1976 movie *Buffalo Bill and the Indians?*

2. Ralph Bellamy portrayed President Franklin D. Roosevelt in the 1960 movie *Sunrise at Campobello,* but who portrayed First Lady Eleanor Roosevelt?

3. What popular actress played the title role in the 1981 TV movie *Jacqueline Bouvier Kennedy?*

4. Who portrayed First Lady Mary Todd Lincoln in the 1930 movie *Abraham Lincoln,* starring Walter Huston as the sixteenth President?

5. Who portrayed First Lady Edith Wilson in the 1944 motion picture *Wilson,* which starred Alexander Knox as President Wilson'?

6. Celeste Holm portrayed what First Lady in the 1979 TV miniseries *Backstairs at the White House?*

7. Academy Award–winning actress Estelle Parsons portrayed what First Lady opposite Harry Morgan in the 1979 TV miniseries *Backstairs at the White House?*

8. Jane Alexander, MacKenzie Phillips, and Eileen Heckart have all portrayed what First Lady in films?

9. In what 1975 movie did Jacqueline Bissett play Liz Cassidy, a character loosely based on First Lady Jacqueline Kennedy?

10. What actress portrayed First Lady Eleanor Roosevelt in two made-for-television movies, *Eleanor and Franklin* (1976) and *Eleanor and Franklin: The White House Years* (1977)?

QUIZ 60: FIRSTS _____

1. Who was the first President to earn $100,000 a year as the Chief Executive?

2. On February 14, 1849, Mathew Brady photographed what president for the first official Presidential picture?

3. Who was the first President born after the American Revolution?

4. Who was the first left-handed President?

5. Who was the first President to play host to a European monarch at the White House?

6. Who was the first President who did not serve in the Continental Congress or in the U.S. Congress?

7. Who became the first President by appointment, and not elected by the people?

8. What President was the first man to defeat two former Presidents in the same election?

9. Name the President who became the first member of Congress to enlist in the service during World War II.

10. Who was the first log cabin President?

Extra. Who was the first President against whom an impeachment attempt was undertaken by the Congress?

QUIZ 61: THE FLAG _____

1. What President ordered the American flag flown over the White House and also suggested that it be flown over the country's schools?

2. During whose administration was the flag established as consisting of thirteen horizontal red and white stripes with white stars for each state in a field of blue?

3. Francis Scott Key wrote "The Star Spangled Banner" about the American flag at Fort McHenry at Baltimore. Fort McHenry was named after what President's Secretary of War, James McHenry?

4. Who was serving as President on May 29, 1916, when the official Presidential flag was adopted?

5. Who was the first Vice President to feature the official Vice Presidential flag established by executive order #7285?

Extra. On July 6, 1971, what President signed the order establishing that fifty U.S. flags be placed around the base of the Washington Monument and that they wave both day and night?

Extra. Who was serving as President when the United States flag received its forty-ninth and fiftieth stars in January 1959?

QUIZ 62: FOOD AND DRINK _____

1. What President created Chicken à la King?

2. What President began many of his days by drinking a quart of hard cider?

3. What President was presented with a 1400-pound block of cheddar cheese at his White House reception?

4. What First Lady was nicknamed Lemonade Lucy after she banned alcoholic beverages from the White House?

5. What President is credited with being the first man in America to grow a tomato?

6. What President enjoyed the soft drink, Fresca, so much that he had special taps installed in the White House?

7. What President is credited with introducing macaroni to America?

8. What President introduced the waffle to America when he imported the first waffle iron from Holland?

9. What President ran up a wine bill of $10,835.90 during his eight years in the White House?

10. When Chinese Ambassador Li Hung-Chang served Chop Suey at a party, what President was present and became the first Chief Executive to taste the dish?

QUIZ 63: FOOTBALL _____

1. What college named after two Presidents became the first college to feature uniform numbers on their players' jerseys?

2. What President wore uniform #33 while he played guard for Eureka College's Golden Tornadoes?

3. What President was injured during a West Point football game when he attempted to tackle Jim Thorpe?

4. When he played college football, what President was offsides on many of the plays in which he was involved?

5. What President once said of Gerald Ford that "he played too much football with his helmet off"?

6. What President threatened to outlaw football in 1905 because too many young men were getting killed on the gridiron?

7. After failing to make his college football team what President then became a cheerleader?

8. What President was offered a pro football contract with both the Green Bay Packers and the Detroit Lions?

9. What President seriously injured his back while playing football at Harvard University?

10. For the 1971 Super Bowl, President Richard M. Nixon sent Miami Dolphins coach Don Shula a play to have what player run a down-and-out pattern?

Extra. What football player did President Ronald Reagan portray in the 1940 movie *Knute Rockne, All-American?*

QUIZ 64: FORMER PRESIDENTS _____

1. How many Presidents have served in office while there were no other former Presidents alive?

2. Who was the first President who did not attend the inauguration of his successor?

3. Name the three Presidents, each running on a minor party ticket, who were defeated in their bid for the Presidency.

4. What President lived the shortest time (103 days) after leaving the Presidency?

5. Between March 4, 1933, and March 4, 1953, a period of twenty years, there was only one former President alive. Name him.

Extra. Name the President who took over the rectorship of the University of Virginia upon the death of Thomas Jefferson.

QUIZ 65: FUNERALS _____

1. What soldier gave the eulogy at the funeral of President George Washington in 1799?

2. Who was the first President buried in Arlington National Cemetery?

3. Anita Bryant sang "The Battle Hymn of the Republic" at the funeral of which President?

4. President Franklin D. Roosevelt's funeral train traveled through Washington, D.C., but where did the train begin and end?

5. What Speaker of the House's funeral was attended by President John F. Kennedy and former Presidents Dwight D. Eisenhower and Harry S Truman?

6. Who was the first President to lie in state in the Capitol rotunda?

7. Of the twenty-five people who have lain in state in the Capitol rotunda, the only related men were one President and (later) his son. Name the President.

8. Who was the only President to give the eulogy of another President (on May 30, 1969)?

9. Who was the second President to be buried in Arlington National Cemetery?

10. What President had three funerals—one in Elberon, New Jersey, the second in Washington, D.C., and the third in Cleveland, Ohio?

QUIZ 66: GOVERNORS _____

1. What President served as the governor of the state of New Jersey?

2. During his eight years as governor, who signed the biggest tax increase in the history of California?

3. In 1979 what President succeeded Henry Clay as governor of Virginia?

4. In 1803 what President dueled with Tennessee governor John Sevier?

5. What two Presidents were both the sons of governors of Virginia?

6. Of which state did President John Tyler previously serve as governor?

7. Both Theodore Roosevelt and Franklin D. Roosevelt served as governor of what state?

8. What future President was elected governor of Tennessee after serving as the Speaker of the House of Representatives?

9. What governor of Tennessee and President once made a suit of clothes for the governor of Kentucky?

10. What President was the first governor of Ohio to be elected for three terms?

11. What governor and President once lost a gubernatorial election to Lester Maddox?

12. President Theodore Roosevelt selected what President to serve as the first governor of the Philippines?

13. Richard M. Nixon unsuccessfully ran for governor of what state in 1962?

14. What President was elected governor of New York only to give up the office to serve as the Secretary of State under Andrew Jackson?

15. Grover Cleveland unsuccessfully ran for governor of which state?

16. President William McKinley served two terms as the governor of what state?

17. Who served as the first territorial governor of Florida in 1821?

18. Name the only President to serve as a territorial governor of the Indiana Territory.

19. Only two Presidents have served as military governors. Name both men who share the same initials.

20. What Vice President set a record when he served seven terms as governor of the state of New York?

QUIZ 67: GRANDFATHERS— GRANDSONS _____

1. Which Vice President's grandson was defeated twice for the Presidency?

2. What President became a grandfather when his grandson, James Madison Randolph, was the first child born in the White House?

3. In 1842 which President's granddaughter became the first girl to be born in the White House?

4. Only one grandfather and grandson combination have been elected to serve as Presidents of the United States. Name both men.

5. The grandson of which President was the inspiration for the name of a Presidential retreat?

6. The grandfather of which Vice President served as the first president of the College of New Jersey (Princeton)?

7. What President fought in the Civil War, as his grandfather had fought in the War of 1812, and as his great-grandfather had fought in the Revolutionary War?

8. Which child of President Ronald Reagan made him a grandfather for the first time in 1979?

9. Which President's grandson (George Wythe Randolph) served as the first Secretary of War for the Confederacy?

10. The granddaughter (Elizabeth) of which President married Navy Captain Alfred Hart Miles, the cowriter (lyrics) of the Navy hymn "Anchors Aweigh"?

11. James Taylor was the great-grandfather of which two Presidents?

12. The grandson (John Taylor Wood) of which President was on board the *Merrimac* during its battle with the *Monitor*?

13. Charles Francis Adams III, the great-grandson of President John Quincy Adams, served as the Secretary of which department under President Herbert Hoover?

14. Which President's great-grandfather George crossed the Delaware River with George Washington during the American Revolution?

15. Josephine May Hannon Fitzgerald was the only grandmother to be able to vote for her grandson for the Presidency. For whom did she vote?

Extra. Which President's paternal grandfather was killed by Indians in 1782?

QUIZ 68: HABITS AND TRAITS _____

1. What President required an average of eleven hours of sleep each night?

2. Name the superstitious President who often made announcements on the thirteenth of the month and considered the number lucky.

3. What President is said to have smoked twenty cigars each day?

4. Who was the first President with the habit of smoking cigarettes?

5. What President often enjoyed munching on jelly beans during White House meetings?

QUIZ 69: HANDICAPS _____

1. Although a well-kept secret at the time, what President was blinded in his left eye after having been struck during a boxing match in 1904?

2. What President's poor eyesight kept him out of combat during World War II?

3. What President was injured while playing football, causing a back problem which plagued him the remainder of his life?

4. As a result of a childhood accident, the right arm of which President was smaller than his left arm?

5. What handicap did Julia, the wife of Ulysses S. Grant, have that the President would not let her correct because he liked her that way?

Extra. What President carried a bullet in his chest the rest of his life that he received in a duel with Charles Dickinson, whom he had shot and killed?

Extra. What President wore a hearing aid in both his ears?

QUIZ 70: HEALTH _____

1. In 1893 what President secretly underwent cancer surgery in which part of his upper jaw was removed?

2. What President had an epileptic wife?

3. What President became disabled after he suffered a paralytic stroke on September 26, 1919?

4. What President suffered a nervous breakdown at the age of twenty-two and recovered in a sanitarium?

5. From which chronic illness did President Abraham Lincoln suffer?

6. What President had to be tutored as a child because he was too sickly to attend a regular school?

7. Who was the only President confined to a wheel chair as a result of contracting polio at the age of thirty-nine?

8. Abraham Lincoln was suffering a mild case of what disease when he gave his famous Gettysburg Address in November 1863?

9. What former war hero suffered from tuberculosis while serving as the President?

10. What President underwent an operation to remove a bullet that he carried in his body from a gun fired twenty years earlier by Jesse Benton, the brother of Thomas Hart Benton?

Extra. What President and what First Lady were issued Medicare cards number one and two?

QUIZ 71: HEIGHTS _____

1. Who was the first President under six feet tall?

2. At 5' 4" who was the shortest President?

3. At 6' 4" who was the tallest President?

4. Which of the two Roosevelts was taller, Theodore or Franklin?

5. Name the President who stood only 5' 3" when he entered college, but left at the height of 5' 10".

6. What President married a woman who was not only taller than he was, but a bit heavier?

7. Who was taller at the Potsdam Conference: President Harry S Truman, Prime Minister Winston Churchill, or Premiere Joseph Stalin?

8. How tall was George Washington?

9. Who was taller—the twenty-second President or the twenty-fourth President of the United States?

10. Who was the last President under six feet tall?

QUIZ 72: HEROISM _____

1. What President claimed to have saved the lives of seventy-seven people over several seasons while serving as a lifeguard?

2. What President rescued the future wife of the Chinese minister to the United States from a house fire when she was just a little girl?

3. During World War II, what President was credited with saving the lives of several of his crew and swam with one man for a distance of three miles?

4. Whose picture is on the Purple Heart medal, which is presented to American soldiers who are wounded in action?

5. Name the son of a President who, while serving as a pilot in Europe, was shot down and killed on July 14, 1918.

6. White House guard Leslie Cofflet was shot and killed in his attempt to protect which President against an assassination attempt?

7. What President dedicated the Hall of Heroes in the Pentagon building in Washington, D.C., to honor Medal of Honor winners?

8. Secret Service agents Rufus Youngblood and Clinton J. Hill were both honored for protecting the Vice President and First Lady during which Presidential assassination?

9. What President often singled out individual American heroes during his State of the Union addresses?

10. What President called Lt. Col. Oliver North a hero after he had just been fired from the White House?

QUIZ 73: HISTORY ─────────────────

1. All the men who ever walked on the moon did so during the administration of which President?

2. What President sent out the Lewis and Clark Expedition to explore the Northwest?

3. Under which President was the first income tax law passed?

4. The cousin of which President organized the famous Boston Tea Party on the night of December 16, 1773?

5. Under which President was the size of the United States doubled?

QUIZ 74: HOBBIES _____

1. Who was the first President to grow *Cannabis sativa* (marijuana)?

2. What President and his wife were the first couple to ban drinking and dancing at the White House?

3. A former tailor, who was the first President to make his own clothing?

4. Although he would die of throat cancer, what President enjoyed smoking upwards of twenty cigars each day?

5. What President enjoyed hunting, camping, fishing, hiking, and going on safari?

6. What President spent $84.50 of his own money to purchase a billiard table and chess set for the White House?

7. What did Thomas Jefferson plan to install in the dome of Monticello until it was outlawed in Virginia?

8. What President owned a number of roosters that he used in the sport of cockfighting?

9. What President played poker weekly with members of his cabinet?

10. What was President John Adams's lifelong hobby?

QUIZ 75: HOLIDAYS _____

1. Thomas Jefferson and James Knox Polk both married their wives on which same holiday?

2. In Plymouth, Vermont, in 1845 who became the only President to be born on the Fourth of July?

3. On May 16, 1920, who was the only Vice President to die on his birthday?

4. Name the two Presidents who both died on Independence Day, July 4, 1826.

5. How many Presidents' birthdays are federal holidays?

6. Name the two Presidents who married on their birthdays.

7. President John Adams's grandson, also named John Adams, was born on the same day of the year on which his grandfather died. What day was it?

8. What President declared the nation's first bank holiday?

9. Although it didn't last, what was the first holiday in the United States?

10. Who served as President in 1886, for the Centennial celebration of the United States?

Extra. Name President Abraham Lincoln's Vice President who died on July 4, 1891.

Extra. The daughter (Julia) of which President was born on the Fourth of July?

QUIZ 76: HOLLYWOOD _____

1. What President subscribed to the *Hollywood Reporter* and had it delivered to his Oval Office desk each day?

2. What Hollywood actress, born Dorothy Gatley, borrowed her screen name from President Warren G. Harding?

3. What President was buried in Hollywood?

4. What Hollywood actor in films and TV coached Presidents Dwight D. Eisenhower, Richard Nixon, and Gerald Ford on how to conduct themselves on television?

5. What actress sang "Happy Birthday" to President John F. Kennedy at a Democratic fund-raiser in Madison Square Garden on March 19, 1962, just prior to his forty-fifth birthday?

6. What actress sang "Happy Birthday" to President John F. Kennedy at New York's Waldorf-Astoria Hotel on his forty-sixth birthday?

7. In 1939 the son of which President became the vice president of Goldwyn Pictures under Samuel Goldwyn?

8. Of what Hollywood union did Ronald Reagan once serve as president?

9. What former president of the Screen Actors Guild often applied President Dwight D. Eisenhower's makeup whenever he appeared on television?

10. Hollywood has featured what President in more films than any other Chief Executive?

QUIZ 77: HOMES _____

1. The home of which President at 380 Mount Vernon Avenue in Marion, Ohio, is a museum?

2. What President resided at 1 Cherry Street and also in a house on Broadway in New York City?

3. What President lived with his First Lady in the Octagon House while the White House was being rebuilt?

4. In what official government residence did President Harry S Truman and his family reside while the White House was being refurbished?

5. Name the seven Presidents who were born in log cabins.

6. What President's boyhood home in Louisville, Kentucky, was named Springfield?

7. Other than Washington, D.C., what other cities have been home to executive mansions?

8. Who was the only President to make Washington, D.C., his home after he left the White House?

9. The Tennessee home of which President's wife was considered neutral territory by both the North and the South during the Civil War?

10. Hyde Park, New York, was the home of the family of which President?

QUIZ 78: HONORS _____

1. What President was once given the title of "Father of the Year"?

2. What President turned down an honorary degree from Oxford University because he felt that he did not warrant the honor?

3. What President signed the bill that created the Congressional Medal of Honor?

4. When John Quincy Adams lost the Presidential election in 1828, what did the town of Adams, New Hampshire, change its name to?

5. John Quincy Adams made the following remark when his alma mater, Harvard University, conferred a Doctor of Law degree upon which President: "Myself an affectionate child of our alma mater, I would not be present to witness her disgrace in conferring her highest literary honors upon a barbarian who could not write a sentence of grammar and hardly could spell his own name"?

6. In 1900, who became the first person selected by New York University's Hall of Fame of Great Americans?

7. Who was the first President since Franklin D. Roosevelt not to be chosen as *Time* magazine's "Man of the Year"?

8. What President had a newly discovered astroid named in his honor?

9. What dam on the Colorado River was named for a President, then renamed Boulder Dam, then renamed for that President?

10. As a young Representative what President was named "Washington's Gay Young Bachelor"?

11. Who was the only President depicted on a U.S. coin during his lifetime?

12. What President has been given more honorary degrees (eighty-nine) than any other American?

13. What President was personally decorated by General Douglas MacArthur during World War II?

14. What President had a plant named in his honor?

15. What President inspired the name of a toy animal that is still popular today?

QUIZ 79: HORSES _____

1. George Washington rode what horse at Cornwallis's surrender at Yorktown?

2. What President as a soldier rode a horse named Egypt?

3. What President rode a mount called the General in battle?

4. What President had two horses shot from under him during a battle on the same day, July 9, 1755?

5. What President owned a racehorse named Greylord on which he won $6500 in bets?

6. What was the name of the pony that the Roosevelt boys took to the second floor of the White House?

7. What President rode such horses as Little Man and Sinbad?

8. What was the name of Caroline Kennedy's pet pony?

9. What President's favorite horse, Whitey, served at his master's funeral parade?

10. Black Jack appeared in 1963, and again in 1973 as the riderless horse at the funeral processions of which two Presidents?

QUIZ 80: HOUSE OF REPRESENTATIVES —

1. Name the four Presidents who served in the House of Representatives during 1833 and 1834.

2. Name the three Presidents who served in the House of Representatives in 1947 and 1948.

3. What President first came to Washington, D.C., in 1932 as a secretary to Congressman Richard M. Kleberg?

4. Who was the only President to serve as Speaker of the House?

5. Who was the first of eighteen Presidents to serve in the House of Representatives in the first, second, third, and fourth Congresses?

Extra. In 1796, who was elected as Tennessee's first Representative to Congress?

QUIZ 81: INAUGURAL ADDRESSES _____

1. What President gave the longest inauguration speech on record (8,578 words)?

2. Who was the first President to give his inauguration speech outdoors?

3. How many Presidents did not give an inaugural address?

4. What President stated, "And so, my fellow Americans: ask not what your country can do for you, ask what you can do for your country," during his inaugural speech?

5. "The only thing we have to fear is fear itself," was uttered by which President during his inaugural address?

6. Who was the first President to commit his inaugural speech to memory rather than read it?

7. What President mentioned the prophet Micah in his inaugural address?

8. What Vice President took his oath of office and gave his inaugural speech while intoxicated—possibly the only time in his life that he had been drunk?

9. What President used the pronoun "I" a record forty-five times in his 8,445-word inaugural address?

10. What President spoke three more words in his second inaugural address than his first?

QUIZ 82: INAUGURAL BALLS ————————

1. What President's inaugural ball was the most expensive in United States history?

2. Because there was such a great demand for tickets, who was the first President to have more than one inaugural ball?

3. Who was the first President to hold an inaugural ball in Washington, D.C.?

4. Members of the electoral college were invited for the first time to which President's inaugural ball?

5. What First Lady wore the same dress to her husband's inaugural ball in Atlanta that she wore to his Presidential Ball six years later?

Extra. What President held his inaugural ball at the Smithsonian Institution's National Museum of American History?

Extra. What President entered Washington on March 4, 1877, without either an inauguration parade or an inaugural ball?

Extra. What First Lady was buried in the same dress that she wore to her husband's inaugural ball?

QUIZ 83: INAUGURAL PARADES _____

1. What President rode in a wooden model of the frigate *Constitution* during his inaugural Parade?

2. On March 4, 1921, who became the first President to ride to his inauguration in an automobile?

3. Who was the only President to bring his pet dog to his inaugural parade?

4. In 1809 what President-elect led the first inaugural parade in Washington, D.C.?

5. Grandstands were first constructed along Pennsylvania Avenue for the inaugural parade of which President?

6. What President's inauguration featured one of the most spectacular parades in Washington with 35,000 participants including a group of Indians?

7. At which President's inauguration did the Marine Corps Band make its first public appearance?

8. Three elephants and a 280mm atomic cannon were in the inauguration parade of which President?

9. Who became the first First Lady to ride with her husband in his inaugural parade?

10. Who was the first First Lady to take part in her husband's inauguration and parade?

QUIZ 84: INAUGURATIONS _____

1. Who was the first President inaugurated in Washington, D.C.?

2. Who was the first President to have his mother present at his inauguration?

3. Who was the first President inaugurated on the West Front of the Capitol instead of the traditional East Front?

4. What four Presidents attended the 1860 inauguration of President Abraham Lincoln?

5. The second term of which President had the first inauguration held on January 20, rather than on March 4 in accordance with the Twentieth Amendment?

6. The Indian Chief Geronimo was a guest at which Presidential inauguration?

7. Calvin Coolidge and Herbert Hoover were both sworn into office as President by which former President?

8. What President took his oath of office on the steps of the brick Capitol building in Washington's first outdoor inauguration?

9. Who was the only President inaugurated in two different cites? Name the cities.

10. Who were the two Presidents sworn into office in Philadelphia?

QUIZ 85: INITIALS _____

1. What President's middle initial does not stand for any name?

2. Name the four Presidents whose first and last names begin with the same letters.

3. What was President Warren G. Harding's middle name?

4. For what did Ulysses S. Grant's middle initial stand, although he was nicknamed "Unconditional Surrender" Grant?

5. Name President James Buchanan's Vice President and the man that Buchanan defeated for the Presidency, both of whom had the middle initial C.

6. Who were the three Presidents known by their three initials?

7. What was President Chester A. Arthur's middle name?

8. The middle initial A was shared by which two Presidents?

9. Name the two pairs of Presidents who shared the same initials.

10. How many Presidents did not have a middle name or middle initial?

Extra. What President, his wife, and their two children all had the same initials?

Extra. The middle initial D was shared by which two Presidents?

QUIZ 86: IN-LAWS _____

1. What President had four brothers-in-law who fought for the Confederacy during the Civil War?

2. What President was the brother-in-law of a British-born motion picture actor?

3. Name the only President whose father-in-law, David Gardiner, was a United States Senator.

4. What President had his daughter-in-law serve as the mistress of the White House in place of a First Lady?

5. Confederate President Jefferson Davis was the son-in-law of which President of the United States?

6. Actress Faye Emerson became the daughter-in-law of which President when she married his son Elliott?

7. What President's own personal secretary, Samuel Gouverneur, married his youngest daughter, Maria?

8. How many President's fathers-in-law were clergymen?

9. What President was the father-in-law of the grandson of another President?

10. In 1986 what Hollywood actor married Maria Shriver, the daughter of Eunice Kennedy Shriver, who was the sister of President John F. Kennedy?

Extra. What was the name of President John F. Kennedy's brother-in-law whom he appointed in 1961 to head the Peace Corps?

Extra. What President was the father-in-law of his own Secretary of State William G. McAdoo?

QUIZ 87: INVENTIONS _____

1. What President was responsible for inventing the swivel chair?

2. Who was the only President to be issued a patent (#6469) for lifting boats over land?

3. What President helped to form a company that marketed fresh orange juice in plastic bags?

4. With what inventor did President Rutherford B. Hayes talk in 1877 on the very first telephone call made to the White House?

5. What President was related to a man who took inventor Robert J. Fulton to court, claiming that it was he who invented the steamboat, and not Fulton?

QUIZ 88: INVENTIONS OF THOMAS JEFFERSON _____

Which of the following inventions listed were associated with Thomas Jefferson, either as inventor or the person who introduced the invention to America?

A. Swivel chair

B. Stove

C. Lazy Susan

D. Lightning rod

E. Pedometer

F. Folding chair

G. Ballpoint pen

H. Bifocals

I. Hemp machine

J. An improved plow

QUIZ 89: LAND ACQUISITIONS _____

1. During whose administration was the Louisiana Purchase made at a cost of $15 million?

2. Florida was purchased from Spain for the sum of $5 million while which man was President?

3. California became the thirty-first state of the Union during which President's administration?

4. Who was President when the future state of Alaska was purchased from Russia?

5. From what country did President Franklin Pierce negotiate the Gadsden Purchase in 1854?

6. What President's campaign promise was to make Texas a part of the United States?

7. What President in his last Presidential message advocated making Cuba a state of the Union?

8. What other President wanted to buy Cuba from Spain and make it a state?

9. During whose administration did the United States acquire the Philippines, Guam, and Puerto Rico?

10. President Woodrow Wilson approved the purchase of the Canary Islands from what country for the price of $25 million in 1916?

QUIZ 90: LANGUAGES _____

1. What President grew up speaking Dutch?

2. What President addressed the German people in their native tongue, proclaiming, "Ich bin ein Berliner" (I am a Berliner)?

3. What President taught both Greek and Latin at Hiram College?

4. What President had a typewriter that could type in English and in Greek?

5. What President's wife spoke five languages, including Chinese?

6. What President studied American Indian languages and established a list of Indian vocabulary?

7. What President knew how to speak English, Latin, Greek, French, Dutch, and Spanish?

8. What two First Ladies taught their husbands to write English?

9. What First Lady learned to speak German in order to help her husband with his research?

10. What First Lady was married in a Greek Orthodox ceremony conducted in the Greek language?

QUIZ 91: LASTS _____

1. Who was the last President who was neither a Democrat or a Republican?

2. Who was the last President to serve more than two terms in office?

3. Who was the last President to be shot in office?

4. Who was the last President to refuse a salary as President?

5. Who was the last President born in a log cabin?

Extra. Who was the last President to serve without a Vice President?

Extra. Who was the last of five Presidents born in November as well as the last of seven Presidents born in Ohio?

QUIZ 92: LAST WORDS _____

1. "This is the last of earth, I am content" were the final words of which President?

2. "Edith, I'm a broken machine, but I'm ready" were the last words of which President?

3. Knowing he was unpopular, which President uttered these final words: "Doctor, I am going, perhaps, it is best for everyone"?

4. What President said these dying words to his devoted wife: "Sarah, for all eternity, I love you"?

5. Richard Nixon repeated the last words of which President while giving his eulogy?

6. "I always talk better lying down" were the final words of which President?

7. "My God, I've been hit" were the last words uttered by which President before he died from an assassin's bullet?

8. Which President's last words were reported to have been, " 'Tis well"?

9. What President who liked to drink asked ironically for water on his deathbed?

10. Which President's final words were those of the hymn "Nearer My God to Thee"?

11. "This nourishment is palatable" were the final words of which President as he sipped some soup?

12. While posing for a portrait what President uttered his dying words, "I have a terrific headache"?

13. What President said "Please turn out the lights" before he died?

14. Referring to his wife, what President spoke these final words: "I know that I am going where Lucy is"?

15. What dying President spoke these final words to Vice President John Tyler: "Sir, I wish you to understand the true principles of government. I wish them carried out. I ask nothing more"?

QUIZ 93: THE LAW _____

1. What President studied law under Thomas Jefferson?

2. Who was the only President to have testified via videotape in a criminal trial while serving as President?

3. What President once uttered these words: "There are extreme cases when the law become inadequate even to their own preservation, and where the universal resource is a dictator, or martial law"?

4. What President once served as a deputy sheriff in Billings County, Montana?

5. Benjamin Harrison's law partner, David Wallace, was the son of what governor and author?

6. What President won his first lawsuit at the age of sixteen?

7. What President executed a man while he was sheriff of Erie County, New York?

8. Who defended a black woman named Lizzie Jennings, who had been thrown off a trolley car because of her color?

9. What President appointed his brother, William, as a U.S. Marshal to Texas?

10. What President was the prosecuting attorney for Stark County, Ohio?

Extra. Name the President who defended the British soldiers who fired on the crowd during the "Boston Massacre."

QUIZ 94: LEGENDS AND RUMORS _____

1. What famous George Washington legend in which George could not tell a lie was actually created by biographer Parson Weems?

2. Although he was listed as born in Fairfield, Vermont, what President was rumored to have been born in Canada?

3. What President was nicknamed the Beast of Buffalo because he was rumored to beat his wife?

4. Who was the first President rumored to be of black ancestry, to which he replied, "How do I know, one of my ancestors may have jumped the fence"?

5. What President is believed by some historians to have fathered five children by his slave, Sally Hemings, the half-sister of his late wife?

6. According to Allan W. Eckert in his book *The Frontier,* what President was actually born in 1755 on board a ship traveling from Ireland to America?

7. According to the diary of President John Quincy Adams, what President was reported to be the illegitimate son of Vice President Aaron Burr?

8. What President was said to have been poisoned by his wife, Florence, who then refused to let an autopsy be performed on his body?

9. What President suspected that he'd been born illegitimately, as his mother had been?

10. What writer in the *New York Evening Mail* began the fable that President Millard Fillmore had installed the first bathtub in the White House in January 1851?

QUIZ 95: LIBRARIES _____

1. What President read every book in the public library in Independence, Missouri, by the time he was fourteen years old, or so the legend goes?

2. What Presidential library (and burial place) is located in West Branch, Iowa?

3. What President used his own library to begin the first White House library?

4. What President served on a bucket brigade to help put out a fire at the Library of Congress?

5. Ann Arbor, Michigan, is the location of what Presidential library?

6. In what Washington, D.C., museum is Franklin D. Roosevelt's Four Freedom's Library located?

7. The Library of Congress was stocked in 1815 with 6,487 volumes from what President's own personal library?

8. What President unsuccessfully attempted to have the dome of the Library of Congress building torn down because he didn't like its looks?

9. The three buildings of the Library of Congress are each named after a President. Name the three buildings.

10. Where is the original copy of President Abraham Lincoln's Gettysburg Address safely kept?

QUIZ 96: LINCOLN–KENNEDY SIMILARITIES _____

Fill in the blanks:

1. Presidents Abraham Lincoln and John F. Kennedy were both killed on a _____ (day of the week).

2. Both Abraham Lincoln and John F. Kennedy were succeeded by a President named _____.

3. Abraham Lincoln's Vice President Andrew Johnson was born in 1808. John F. Kennedy's Vice President Lyndon Johnson was born in _____.

4. Abraham Lincoln was elected to Congress in 1846. John F. Kennedy was elected to Congress in _____.

5. President Abraham Lincoln defeated Stephen A. Douglas, who was born in 1813. President John F. Kennedy defeated Richard M. Nixon, who was born in _____.

QUIZ 97: LOSERS _____

1. Who spoke the immortal words, "I would rather be right than be President"?

2. What position in United States history does Victoria Claflin Woodhull hold?

3. To whom did John F. Kennedy lose the Democratic Vice Presidential nomination in 1956?

4. In 1966 Ronald Reagan defeated Edmund G. "Pat" Brown to become governor of California. In 1962 who had Brown previously defeated to become governor?

5. Who was the only Supreme Court justice to run for the Presidency although he was defeated by Woodrow Wilson?

Extra. The brother of which President lost in his bid to be elected mayor of Plains, Georgia?

QUIZ 98: MAGAZINES _____

1. What President stated in a *Playboy* magazine interview, "I've committed adultery in my heart many times"?

2. *The President's Mystery Story* was published in *Liberty* magazine before it was released as a book. What President created the idea for the story?

3. The son of which President was a reporter for *Rolling Stone* magazine in the 1980s?

4. Who was the only President since Franklin D. Roosevelt not selected as *Time* magazine's "Man of the Year"?

5. To which magazine did eyewitness Abraham Zapruder sell his film of the assassination of President John F. Kennedy in November 1963?

6. What First Lady wrote the magazine article "If I Were Negro" for *Negro Digest* magazine?

7. Both *Cosmopolitan* and *Look* magazines featured what model and President on their covers?

8. In 1913 what President sued *Iron Age* magazine for libel when they wrote that he was drunk? He won six cents in damages.

9. Edwin T. Meredith, the founder of *Better Homes and Gardens* magazine, served as the Secretary of Agriculture under which President?

10. Whose daughter, Lynda, was a contributing editor to the *Ladies Home Journal?*

Extra. What President appeared on the cover of *Time* magazine a record sixty-four times?

QUIZ 99: MARRIAGES _____

1. Who was the only bachelor President?

2. Who was the only President married within the White House?

3. Who was the first President to remarry while in office when he wed his second wife, Julia Gardiner?

4. What President's twenty-three-year-old fiancée took an overdose of laudanum and died?

5. What else happened to Dwight D. Eisenhower on July 1, 1916, the day on which he married Mamie?

6. What grandson of a President married the daughter of his grandfather's Vice President?

7. What Vice President introduced James Madison to Dolley Todd, his wife-to-be?

8. Who was the youngest President to marry and the only President to marry as a teenager?

9. What President promised his wife on her deathbed that he would never marry again, and kept that promise?

10. What President had two daughters who were married in the White House during his term of office?

11. What President married the niece of his first wife?

12. How many Presidents married widows?

13. How many Presidents were married in New York City?

14. Name the three Presidents who married while in office.

15. What President married twenty-five-year-old Helen "Nellie" Herron, the daughter of John W. Herron, a law partner of former President Rutherford B. Hayes?

16. Who were the two Presidents who waited until their forties before they married?

17. Name the two Presidents who married their wives in London, England.

18. Name the two Presidents who married divorcees.

19. President Andrew Johnson and Eliza McCardle were married on May 5, 1827, by a magistrate who was the first cousin of which President?

20. What three Presidents were married in California?

QUIZ 100: MAYORS _____

1. What President served as the mayor of Buffalo, New York?

2. What President served as mayor of Northhampton, Massachusetts, from 1910 to 1911?

3. The grandfather of which President served as mayor of Boston?

4. What Vice President was elected mayor of Minneapolis in 1945?

5. What President ran for mayor of New York City in 1886 but lost?

6. Anton Cermak, the mayor of what city, was killed during an assassination attempt on President-elect Franklin D. Roosevelt on February 14, 1933, at Bay Front Park, Florida?

7. What President was elected mayor of Greeneville, Tennesse, on three occasions?

8. What mayor of New York City was involved in a conspiracy to kidnap and kill President George Washington?

9. What President was nicknamed the Veto Mayor?

10. The youngest son of which President served as mayor of Cincinnati?

QUIZ 101: MEETINGS _____

1. What three world leaders met at the Yalta Conference in 1945?

2. What three world leaders met at Potsdam on August 10, 1945?

3. Where on August 23, 1944, did President Franklin D. Roosevelt and representatives of the Allies first meet to design the preliminary structure of the United Nations?

4. Where did President Jimmy Carter, Anwar Sadat, and Menachem Begin meet for thirteen days to draw up the Middle East Peace Accords in 1978?

5. In what Italian city did President Ronald Reagan meet with the heads of the European countries for the 1987 Economic Summit?

QUIZ 102: MILITARY _____

1. On August 25, 1814, while British troops were attacking Washington, D.C., who became the only President to actively exercise his authority as commander in chief of the military?

2. As a soldier, George Washington had what fort built near Union, Pennsylvania, in 1754?

3. What President held the lowest military rank of any President?

4. What President became a general in the Union army at the age of thirty?

5. What President once commanded a million men, representing twelve nations, the largest army in the history of warfare?

6. Who was William McKinley's commanding officer during the Civil War?

7. What President was instrumental in founding the U.S. Marine Corps in 1798?

8. Who was the only President to serve as commander in chief after completing his term as President?

9. Name one of the two generals under whom Ulysses S. Grant served during the Mexican War. One lost the Presidency and the other won it.

10. Who were the first two men to hold the rank of lieutenant general?

11. Under which President were one thousand American advisors first sent to South Vietnam?

12. Name the three consecutive Presidents who were generals in the army, Republicans, had middle names, and were born in Ohio.

13. What President was the first soldier to outrank George Washington?

14. Who was the only President to have been a prisoner of war?

15. What President's rank of five-star general was reinstated upon the completion of his term as President?

QUIZ 103: MINORITIES _____

1. President Theodore Roosevelt became the first President to invite a black man to the White House. Who was he?

2. What President appointed Thurgood Marshall as the first black to sit on the Supreme Court?

3. What First Lady resigned from the Daughters of the American Revolution when they refused to allow black singer Marion Anderson to sing at their hall?

4. What President appointed Oveta Culp Hobby to serve as the first Secretary of the Department of Health, Education, and Welfare?

5. What was the name of the first woman to sit on the Supreme Court, who was appointed to that position by President Ronald Reagan?

6. Blacks took part in which President's inaugural parade for the first time?

7. The first black musician to play at a Presidential inauguration played for what newly elected President?

8. Who was the first woman considered for nomination to the Presidency by a major party?

9. What President chose Robert C. Weaver as the first black to serve in a cabinet position as Secretary of Housing and Urban Development (HUD)?

10. Patricia Harris was appointed the first black female cabinet member when what President appointed her to head HUD?

QUIZ 104: MISTAKES _____

1. During Richard M. Nixon's "Checkers" speech he erroneously stated that his wife, Pat, was born on what day?

2. What Presidential candidate erroneously stated that "Poland is not under Soviet domination" during a debate?

3. What President made so many false statements that they became the subject of a book?

4. What President erroneously stated on his deathbed, "Thomas Jefferson still survives," referring to Thomas Jefferson who had died earlier that day?

5. President Abraham Lincoln ironically stated that "The world will little note, nor long remember what we say here . . ." in what famous speech?

QUIZ 105: MONEY _____

1. What President was instrumental in convincing Congress to adopt a decimal monetary system instead of the British system?

2. What President never drew his salary while serving in the White House but collected it after he retired?

3. Who was the only President to decline a salary and instead bill Congress for his expenses?

4. What President was so poor that in April 1841 he had to borrow money to attend his own inauguration in Washington?

5. What was the annual salary of President Ronald Reagan?

6. What was the annual salary of each President from George Washington through Ulysses S. Grant's first term of office?

7. During Ulysses S. Grant's second term of office, Congress increased the President's salary to what amount which lasted through President Theodore Roosevelt's term?

8. President William Howard Taft became the first President to receive what new annual salary?

9. Harry S Truman was the first President to receive what annual salary?

10. Who was the first President to receive an annual salary of $200,000?

Extra. Until Congress decided it was the government's responsibility to pay pensions to several widows of former Presidents, what person had been donating money to several former First Ladies?

Extra. What President once offered Spain $100 million dollars to purchase Cuba only to be turned down?

Extra. What two wealthy Presidents donated their Presidential salaries to charity?

QUIZ 106: MONUMENTS/MEMORIALS ___

1. Name the Presidents carved on Mount Rushmore by Gutzon Borglum.

2. In the state of Missouri stands a monument to which President-for-a-Day?

3. Whose tomb bears the inscription, "Now he belongs to the ages"?

4. For which President was a National Memorial Park named in North Dakota?

5. What President dedicated the cornerstone of the Jefferson Memorial in Washington, D.C., and then returned to dedicate the monument itself?

6. Situated in the Potomac River, My Lord's Island in Washington, D.C., was renamed in honor of which President?

7. The Grant Memorial in Washington, D.C., was sculpted by Henry Shrady, the son of Dr. George Shrady, the doctor who attended to which President before his death?

8. Thirteen Civil War heroes are memorialized in Washington, D.C., but how many Presidents have monuments in the District of Columbia?

9. Architect Henry Bacon was inspired by the Parthenon in Athens, Greece, when he designed what Presidential memorial in 1911?

10. The son of which President has the only memorial located on Capitol Hill?

QUIZ 107: MOTHERS _____

1. The mother of which President served in India with the Peace Corps?

2. The mother of which President spent time in a Union internment camp with her family during the Civil War?

3. Nancy Hanks was the illegitimately born mother of which President?

4. Who was the first President whose mother could have voted for him for President?

5. Who was the first President whose mother survived him and lived to the age of seventy-five?

6. The mother of which President was the first mother to see her son's inauguration?

7. What President called his mother and father "Sallie and Popsie"?

8. What President's adopted first name was his mother's maiden name?

9. Name the seven Presidents whose middle names were taken from their mother's maiden names.

10. What President adopted his mother's maiden name as his middle name to replace his real middle name?

QUIZ 108: MOTION PICTURES _____

1. In what 1957 movie did Ronald Reagan and Nancy Davis appear together for the only time?

2. What President supposedly contacted Jack L. Warner of Warner Bros. Pictures to encourage him to film the 1943 movie *Mission To Moscow?*

3. What is the name of Ronald Reagan's brother who has appeared in three motion pictures?

4. How many movies did Ronald Reagan appear in with his first wife, Academy Award–winning actress Jane Wyman?

5. Who was the first President ever to be filmed?

6. What was the title of the first movie shown in the White House?

7. What President once wrote an unsuccessful screenplay based on the USS *Constitution?*

8. What 1976 movie inspired John W. Hinckley, Jr., to attempt to assassinate President Ronald Reagan?

9. What 1945 movie starring Burgess Meredith and Robert Mitchum did President Dwight D. Eisenhower call "the greatest war picture I've ever seen"?

10. The 1956 movie *Friendly Persuasion* was based on the novel written by Jessamyn West about the great-grandparents of which President?

Extra. Name the director of the 1955 movie *Prince of Players* about Edwin Booth, the brother of assassin John Wilkes Booth. The director also wrote political speeches for both John F. Kennedy and Adlai Stevenson.

Extra. What President quoted a line from the Henry Hathaway film *The Desert Fox* when he stated that "victory has a hundred fathers and defeat is an orphan"?

QUIZ 109: MOTTOES AND SLOGANS ___

1. What President was instrumental in having the motto In God We Trust put on the Great Seal of the United States?

2. What President was unsuccessful in attempting to have the motto In God We Trust removed from U.S. coins?

3. Whose family motto was Exitus acta probat (the end justifies the means)?

4. What President kept a sign on his desk as a senator that quoted Mark Twain, "Always do right; this will gratify some people and astonish the rest"?

5. What President kept a sign on his desk that read "The Buckaroo Stops Here"?

QUIZ 110: MUSIC _____

1. What President claimed that he knew only two songs: "One is 'Yankee Doodle' and the other isn't"?

2. What President used the Academy Award–winning song "High Hopes" for his Presidential campaign song?

3. "The Missouri Waltz" was the favorite song of which Chief Executive?

4. What President was a member of the Princeton Glee Club?

5. What musical instrument did Thomas Jefferson play?

6. Who was serving as President when "The Star-Spangled Banner" was adopted as the official national anthem of the United States?

7. The President's official song, "Hail to the Chief," was first introduced by the Marine Corps Band during which President's administration?

8. What musical instrument did First Lady Abigail Adams bring into the White House at a cost of $458?

9. What President has been the subject of over five hundred songs, the most of any Chief Executive?

10. What President once played trombone with a group called the *Silver Cornet Band?*

QUIZ 111: NAMES _____

1. What was Ulysses S. Grant's Christian name at birth?

2. Name the six Presidents whose first names were James.

3. Name the four Presidents whose first names were John.

4. Name the three Presidents whose first names were William.

5. What was President Grover Cleveland's real first name?

6. What President reversed his first and middle names?

7. What President had no name for the first six weeks of his life?

8. What President went unnamed for the first four months of his life?

9. What President was named for the King of England?

10. What two Presidents were called Tommy as little boys?

11. By what popular name did Theodore Roosevelt prefer to be called?

12. Name the four surnames shared by more than one President.

13. Who was the only President named after another, unrelated President?

14. Who was the only President to enter office with an entirely different name than the one he was born with?

15. Name the President named for his older brother who had died in infancy.

16. What President was named after a minister friend of his father?

17. What Vice President lent his name to a city in Texas?

18. What first name was First Lady Rosalynn Carter given at birth?

19. What first name was First Lady Eleanor Roosevelt given at birth?

Extra. Who was the first President to name his son after a previous President?

QUIZ 112: NATURE _____

1. What President went on an African safari after leaving office?

2. What President had a Wyoming mountain peak named after him?

3. In 1872 President Ulysses S. Grant established the nation's first national park. Name this 2,221,000-acre park.

4. What President worked as a ranger at Yellowstone National Park during the summer of 1936?

5. In 1906 President Theodore Roosevelt established the nation's first national monument. What is the name of that monument?

Extra. What President signed a bill that added 104 million acres of Alaska's wildlife to the nation's wildlife refuge system?

Extra. What two Presidents have mountain peaks named after them in Alaska?

QUIZ 113: THE NAVY _____

1. What President was talked out of joining the British Navy by his brother Lawrence?

2. Name the only President to serve six years in the U.S. Navy with part of his tour on board a nuclear submarine.

3. Who was President Franklin D. Roosevelt's Secretary of the Navy who was the grandfather of actor Mark Harmon?

4. Who was President Franklin D. Roosevelt's Secretary of the Navy who committed suicide after a nervous breakdown and after whom an aircraft carrier is named?

5. During which President's administration was the Navy Department created in 1798?

6. John P. Kennedy served as the second Secretary of the Navy under which President?

7. What fifty-four-year-old President married the twenty-year-old daughter of his Secretary of the Navy, Thomas W. Gilmer?

8. John J. Bonaparte, President Theodore Roosevelt's Secretary of the Navy, was the grandson of the brother of what French ruler?

9. Charles Francis Adams, the great-grandson of President John Quincy Adams, was the Secretary of the Navy under which President?

10. Name the five consecutive Presidents who served in the U.S. Navy.

QUIZ 114: NEXT-IN-LINE _____

Put in descending order those persons who would be next-in-line to the Presidency:

A. Secretary of Agriculture

B. Secretary of Transportation

C. Secretary of State

D. Secretary of the Interior

E. Secretary of the Treasury

F. Secretary of Commerce

G. President Pro Tempore of the Senate

H. Secretary of Health and Human Services

I. Secretary of Education

J. Secretary of Defense

K. Secretary of Energy

L. Secretary of Labor

M. Secretary of Housing and Urban Development

N. Speaker of the House

O. Attorney General

P. Vice President

QUIZ 115: NICKNAMES #1 _____

1. His Roundness and His Rotundity were two nicknames for what 250-pound, 5' 7" President?

2. What 6' 2" President was nicknamed the Red Fox because of his bright red hair?

3. Who was called the Father of the Constitution?

4. What President was nicknamed Dutch as a boy because his father thought that he looked like a small Dutchman?

5. Who was the first President to use his nickname on official documents?

6. Andrew Jackson was nicknamed Old Hickory; who was nicknamed Young Hickory?

7. After which President were the shantytowns of the Great Depression named?

8. What President was nicknamed Jack?

9. What President dubbed President John Tyler His Accidency when Tyler came to power after the death of President William Henry Harrison?

10. What popular nickname did President Franklin D. Roosevelt give to presidential nominee Alfred E. Landon?

QUIZ 116: NICKNAMES #2 _____

Match the nicknames to the appropriate President:

1. Handsome Frank   A. Calvin Coolidge

2. The Magician   B. Theodore Roosevelt

3. Hero of San Juan Hill   C. John Tyler

4. His Accidency   D. Richard M. Nixon

5. Old Hickory   E. John Adams

6. Iron Butt   F. Abraham Lincoln

7. His Rotundity   G. Martin Van Buren

8. Silent Cal   H. Thomas Jefferson

9. Rail Splitter   I. Franklin Pierce

10. Sage of Monticello   J. Andrew Jackson

QUIZ 117: NOMINATIONS _____

1. What President is considered the darkest horse ever nominated?

2. What city has been the site of ten Presidential nominations, the most of any city?

3. When Henry Gassaway Davis of West Virginia was nominated for President in St. Louis in July 1904, what record was set?

4. Who was the first Presidential candidate to be present at his party's convention to accept the nomination?

5. At the 1880 Republican convention what President was nominated on the thirty-sixth ballot but did not receive a single vote on the first ballot?

Extra. At the age of thirty-six, who was the youngest man to be nominated for the Presidency by a major party?

Extra. In 1856 both the Know-Nothing Party and the Whig Party nominated what same candidate for the Presidency?

Extra. Who was the first Catholic candidate to be nominated for the Presidency by the Democratic Party?

QUIZ 118: NUMBERS _____

1. How many people did Ronald Reagan claim to have saved from drowning in his autobiography, *Where's The Rest of Me?*

2. How many Presidents have died in office?

3. How many Presidents wore beards?

4. How many colleges have been named after President George Washington?

5. What President once shot two hundred and ninty-six animals during an eleven-month period?

6. How many words are in the Presidential oath of office?

7. How many Presidents are not buried in the United States?

8. What President issued Executive Order number one?

9. What President was involved in three different elections which he lost by one vote in each?

10. Who was both the eighth Vice President and the eighth President of the United States?

Extra. Who was both the tenth Vice President and the tenth President of the United States?

QUIZ 119: OATHS _____

1. What President added the words "under God" to the Pledge of Allegiance?

2. What two words can be substituted for each other in the Presidential Oath?

3. Who in 1853 became the first President to use "affirm" in his oath of office, rather than "swear"?

4. Who was the only Vice President to take his oath of office in a foreign country, Cuba, an act which was authorized by a special act of Congress?

5. With what four words did Ronald Reagan complete the Presidential Oath in 1981?

6. What two Presidents did former President William Howard Taft swear into office while he was Chief Justice of the Supreme Court?

7. Where can the Presidential Oath be found in the Constitution?

8. Who was sworn in as the thirty-third President of the United States using a Gideon Bible?

9. Where did Lyndon B. Johnson first take the oath of office for the Presidency?

10. Who does the Constitution designate to administer the oath of office to the President-elect?

11. Who was the only President to take the oath of office from an Associate Justice of the Supreme Court?

12. What Chief Justice officiated at a record nine inaugurations?

13. What two Presidents took the oath of office in New York City?

14. What distant cousin of John Marshall did the Chief Justice swear into office in 1800?

15. Who was the only President to take the oath of office in the same room he where would die?

QUIZ 120: OCCUPATIONS #1 _____

Match each President with his occupation before he became Chief
Executive:

1. Mapmaker   A. Ronald Reagan

2. Tailor   B. Warren G. Harding

3. Mining engineer   C. Woodrow Wilson

4. Fashion model   D. Abraham Lincoln

5. Haberdasher   E. Lyndon B. Johnson

6. Newspaper editor   F. Herbert Hoover

7. Sportscaster   G. Gerald Ford

8. University professor   H. George Washington

9. Ferry operator   I. Harry S Truman

10. Secretary   J. Andrew Jackson

QUIZ 121: OCCUPATIONS #2 _____

1. Who was the first President who was neither a lawyer nor a soldier?

2. What President worked as a janitor while attending college?

3. What President worked for a time in a Nevada City gold mine and a gold mine in Australia?

4. What two Presidents were postmasters?

5. Who was the only President to have been a collector for the Internal Revenue Service?

Extra. Name the five Presidents who were generals during the Civil War.

QUIZ 122: ONLY ⸻

1. Who was the only President to have impeachment proceedings brought against him?

2. Who was the only President who did not live in the White House?

3. Who was the only divorced man elected President of the United States?

4. Who was the only President to resign his office as President?

5. Name the only President born in New Jersey.

6. Who was the only President to succeed and be succeeded by the same President?

7. Who was the only President to serve in both World War I and World War II?

8. Who was the only Vice President to defeat his President who was running for re-election?

9. Who was the only President to serve in both the Revolutionary War and the War of 1812?

10. Who was the only President to have been a representative, senator-elect, and a President-elect, all at the same time?

Extra. Who was the only President to father an only child?

Extra. Who was the only First Lady to serve in an executive capacity as a delegate to the United Nations General Assembly?

QUIZ 123: OPPONENTS _____

1. Who was the Democratic nominee for President twice defeated by Dwight D. Eisenhower in 1952 and in 1956?

2. Who was the only man to run against Franklin D. Roosevelt for the Presidency four times?

3. Williams Jennings Bryan twice opposed what President for the Presidency?

4. Name both of Woodrow Wilson's Republican opponents, one in the election of 1912 and the other in 1916, who later became Chief Justices of the Supreme Court.

5. What Vice President ran against his own President for his party's nomination at the Democratic National Convention in 1940?

QUIZ 124: ORGANIZATIONS _____

1. Who was the first President to be a member of the Phi Beta Kappa?

2. Who was the first Eagle Scout to become President?

3. What President was a dishwasher at the Tau Kappa Epsilon fraternity house at Eureka College?

4. What President always wore his American Legion button on his lapel?

5. Who was the first Boy Scout to be elected President?

6. What President became the chairman of the Boys Clubs of America in 1936?

7. What President served as president of the American Bar Association?

8. How many Presidents were members of the Masons?

9. Who was the first President to be a member of the Masons?

10. Who was the only President to become a thirty-three degree Mason?

QUIZ 125: OTHER PEOPLE _____

1. William Herndon was the law partner of which President?

2. Eddie Jacobson was the haberdashery partner of which President?

3. In 1939 Phyllis Brown posed for twenty-one pictures for *Look* magazine with which future President?

4. U.S. Army Surgeon General Joseph K. Barnes attended to which two Presidents after each was shot?

5. In what capacity did Thomas O'Neil serve under President Franklin Pierce?

6. What was John Scott Harrison's unique claim to fame?

7. What man shot a future President and then became the father-in-law of a Presidential candidate?

8. FBI Chief J. Edgar Hoover served under nine different Presidents beginning with whom?

9. To whom did President Richard M. Nixon give his resignation as the President of the United States?

10. Jack Armstrong's sole claim to fame was when what President once beat him in a wrestling match?

QUIZ 126: OTHER PRESIDENTS _____

1. How many Presidents presided over the Continental Congress from 1774 to 1789, before George Washington became the first President of the United States?

2. Who was the first President of the Continental Congress?

3. Who was the first President of the Continental Congress to serve under the Articles of Confederation?

4. What Supreme Court Justice served as President of the Continental Congress?

5. What President of the Continental Congress was the first signer of the Declaration of Independence?

6. Who is considered to have been the legal President of the United States for one day, between President James Knox Polk's last day of office and the swearing in of Zachary Taylor?

7. On March 4, 1877, while President Rutherford B. Hayes was taking over for President Ulysses S. Grant, what senator from Michigan was technically President for a twenty-four hour period?

8. President Andrew Johnson missed being convicted during his impeachment by only one vote. If he had been forced to step down as President who would have served as the next President?

9. On September 5, 1836, who was elected first President of the Republic of Texas?

10. Who served as President of the Confederate States of America?

QUIZ 127: OVAL OFFICE _____

1. In 1878 what world leader presented President Rutherford B. Hayes with a desk that has been used by numerous Presidents ever since?

2. What did the sign read on President Harry S Truman's Oval Office desk?

3. Who was the first President to have a telephone on his Oval Office desk?

4. Who was the first President with a hot line to Moscow available to him in the Oval Office?

5. Who was the first President to use the Presidential Seal?

QUIZ 128: PAINTINGS/PORTRAITS _____

1. What President said, "That's the ugliest thing I've ever seen" when he first saw his official portrait by Pete Hurd?

2. When Jimmy Carter was governor of Georgia he had several portraits of black leaders hung in the state capitol portrait gallery. Which was the first one that he himself hung?

3. President Calvin Coolidge had hairs added to the head of which President's portrait so that his head would not reflect a white glow?

4. Who rescued Gilbert Stuart's portrait of George Washington from the White House in 1814 before the British could burn it?

5. What President painted a portrait of President Abraham Lincoln based on an 1863 photograph?

6. What artist created a famous painting of Franklin D. Roosevelt's "Four Freedoms"?

7. What artist was painting President Franklin D. Roosevelt's portrait in Warm Springs on April 12, 1945, the day of his death?

8. In 1857 what President was authorized by Congress to buy portraits of five former Presidents for $5,000 to put in the White House?

9. Who painted the portrait of George Washington used on the $1 bill?

10. Where is the only portrait of First Lady Eleanor Roosevelt painted from life located?

Extra. What First Lady returned to the White House eight years after leaving it in order to view portraits of her husband and herself?

QUIZ 129: PARDONS _____

1. In 1921 what President pardoned the imprisoned Socialist leader Eugene V. Debs?

2. What President unconditionally pardoned the draft dodgers of the Vietnam War?

3. What President restored United States citizenship to Jefferson Davis?

4. What President pardoned what other President for any crimes he might have committed?

5. In 1980 President Jimmy Carter exonerated what doctor in the death of President Abraham Lincoln?

6. Who did President Jimmy Carter pardon in February 1979?

7. What President pardoned the farmers who took part in the Whiskey Rebellion?

8. The President can pardon offenses against the United States except in what single case?

9. What President later pardoned seven of the black soldiers whom he had ordered dishonorably discharged because they were believed to be involved in a riot in Brownsville, Texas?

10. Who did President Gerald Ford pardon on his final day of office as President?

QUIZ 130: PERSONAL APPEARANCE ____

1. Who was the last President to wear a beard or mustache?

2. Who was the first President to wear a beard?

3. Who was the first President to wear long pants in lieu of the traditional knee breeches?

4. At a peak weight of 352 pounds who was the heaviest President?

5. What President's face was scarred from smallpox?

6. Who was the first President who wore false teeth?

7. What President always went out in public wearing a red carnation in his lapel? (He was fatally shot shortly after he gave his lucky flower away.)

8. What President changed the part in his hair while he was serving as President?

9. What President wore two hearing aids, one in each ear?

10. What President had scars from cuts that a British officer had given him with a saber when he was a boy?

QUIZ 131: PHOTOGRAPHS _____

1. Who was the first President of whom there is a known photograph?

2. Who was the first President photographed at his inauguration?

3. What President was photographed wearing an Indian war bonnet, a picture that became so popular it is still reproduced in history books today?

4. The popular photograph of a dog named King Tut with his master is credited with helping what President win his election?

5. Which President's son filmed the explosion of a Navy PB4Y-1 aircraft in which Joseph P. Kennedy, Jr., was killed during World War II?

6. What was the name of the bystander who filmed the assassination of President John F. Kennedy in Dallas on November 22, 1963?

7. What former First Lady received a court order against photographer Ron Galella to stay at least twenty-five feet away from her and her children?

8. The daughter of which President was employed as a still photographer during the production of the 1978 movie *Jaws 2?*

9. A popular 1940s photograph of President Harry S Truman featured what actress sitting on the top of the upright piano he was playing?

10. Who was the first President photographed in office?

QUIZ 132: PLACES _____

1. Established in 1868, the capital of the African country of Liberia is the only foreign capital named for a U.S. President. Name the capital and the President.

2. What is the only state in the Union named for a U.S. President?

3. After which President was the Brazilian River of Doubt renamed?

4. In what city did President John F. Kennedy introduce himself as the man who had accompanied Jacqueline Kennedy to Europe?

5. What is the name of the only U.S. Presidential landmark located outside of the United States?

Extra. In what state is Mount Rushmore located?

QUIZ 133: POLITICAL OFFICES _____

1. What President was elected the mayor of Greenesville, Tennessee, at the age of twenty-one?

2. What man was elected President after holding just one public office, the governorship of New Jersey, for twenty-two months?

3. What President was employed as a census taker in the state of Missouri?

4. What President held more major offices than any other person?

5. What President first entered politics when he answered a newspaper advertisement looking for candidates?

Extra. In addition to the Presidency, Franklin D. Roosevelt held what same federal office as his fifth cousin Theodore Roosevelt?

QUIZ 134: POLITICAL PARTIES _____

1. To what political party did President George Washington belong?

2. What President changed his political affiliation from Democrat to Republican before he was elected to office?

3. Thomas Jefferson was a member of what political party?

4. Vice President Henry Wallace ran for President on what party ticket in 1948?

5. Only once have the President and the Vice President belonged to two different political parties; one was a Federalist and the other a Republican. Name both men.

6. For what party did President Theodore Roosevelt run for President in 1916 and actually receive more votes than the Republican candidate?

7. Millard Fillmore was defeated in 1856 when he ran as a candidate for what political party?

8. What political party was previously named the Federalists and later called the Republicans?

9. In 1856 who was the first candidate nominated for the Presidency on the Republican ticket, although he did not win?

10. Who was the first Republican to win the Presidency after having previously lost a Presidential campaign?

11. Who served as the first Republican President?

12. Who was the first Democrat elected President?

13. Rufus King in 1816 was the last Presidential candidate to run on what party ticket?

14. In 1831 what political party was the first to hold a national nominating convention?

15. What political party introduced the use of the primaries during the 1840s?

QUIZ 135: POLITICAL SLOGANS _____

1. "Our country, right or wrong!" was a campaign slogan of which President?

2. What Presidential candidate used the political slogan "In your heart you know he's right"?

3. What President offered "A Full Dinner Bucket" as a slogan and a promise?

4. "54° 40′ or fight!" was the rousing Presidential campaign slogan of which President?

5. What President promised "Two chickens in every pot"?

Extra. "Tippecanoe and Tyler Too" was the campaign slogan for the ticket of which President and Vice President?

QUIZ 136: PORTRAITS ON COINS _____

Match the Presidents with the coins on which they are depicted:

1. John F. Kennedy   A. Penny

2. Franklin D. Roosevelt   B. Nickle

3. Abraham Lincoln   C. Dime

4. George Washington   D. Quarter

5. Thomas Jefferson   E. Half-Dollar

6. Dwight D. Eisenhower   F. Dollar

Extra. Who are the only three Presidents depicted on a U.S. coin, paper currency, a savings bond, and a treasury bond?

QUIZ 137: PORTRAITS ON CURRENCY —

Match the Presidents with the currency on which they are depicted:

1. George Washington   A. $2 bill

2. Thomas Jefferson   B. $20 bill

3. Abraham Lincoln   C. $500 bill

4. Andrew Jackson   D. $5000 bill

5. Ulysses S. Grant   E. $1 bill

6. William McKinley   F. $100,000 bill

7. Grover Cleveland   G. $1,000 bill

8. James Madison   H. $50 bill

9. Woodrow Wilson   I. $5 bill

Extra. Who was the only First Lady to have her portrait on U.S. currency?

QUIZ 138: PORTRAITS ON SAVINGS BONDS _____

Match the Presidents with the savings bonds on which they are depicted:

1. Theodore Roosevelt   A. $25

2. Abraham Lincoln   B. $50

3. Woodrow Wilson   C. $75

4. George Washington   D. $100

5. John F. Kennedy   E. $200

6. Grover Cleveland   F. $500

7. Franklin D. Roosevelt   G. $1000

8. Thomas Jefferson   H. $10,000

QUIZ 139: POSTAGE STAMPS _____

1. Postage stamps were first issued in the United States during which Presidential administration?

2. What President was the first American leader to have his picture on a U.S. postage stamp?

3. What two Presidents with the same first name both enjoyed the hobby of collecting postage stamps?

4. The small country of San Marino made what President an honorary citizen and depicted him on one of their stamps?

5. What President did not learn that he was nominated for President by the Whig Party in 1848 because he refused to pay the ten cents due on the COD letter informing him?

6. A month after which President's death in August 1923 did the U.S. Post Office issue a memorial stamp with his picture?

7. The African country of Togo was the first country to feature the portrait of which President on its stamps?

8. The son of which President holds the rare distinction of being only one of two living persons depicted on a U.S. postage stamp?

9. In what year were twenty-nine U.S. postage stamps issued with the portraits of Presidents George Washington through Calvin Coolidge?

10. Of those twenty-nine stamps mentioned in the previous question, what President was featured on the highest denomination—a $5 stamp?

QUIZ 140: PRESIDENTIAL PORTRAYALS

1. Who was the first living President portrayed in a motion picture?

2. Who portrayed President Franklin D. Roosevelt in the 1960 movie *Sunrise at Campobello,* and again in the 1983 TV miniseries *The Winds of War?*

3. What actor played President Theodore Roosevelt in the movies *In Old Oklahoma* (1943), *Buffalo Bill* (1944), and *My Girl Tisa* (1948)?

4. Henry Fonda played the son of which President in the 1962 movie *The Longest Day?*

5. What President was portrayed by Ed Beheler in such movies as *Black Sunday* (1977) and *The Cayman Triangle* (1979)?

Extra. What President was portrayed in the 1976 movie *The Pink Panther Strikes Again* by Dick Crockett, and by Walter Hanna in the 1978 movie *The Bees?*

QUIZ 141: PRESIDENTIAL RELATION-
SHIPS _____

1. President James Madison was the second cousin of which other President?

2. Theodore Roosevelt was a third cousin, twice removed, of which other President?

3. To which two Presidents is Richard M. Nixon related; one a seventh cousin twice removed and the other an eighth cousin once removed?

4. Franklin D. Roosevelt was a fourth cousin once removed of which President?

5. Ulysses S. Grant was a sixth cousin once removed of which President?

Extra. What President was a first cousin twice removed of President George Washington?

Extra. President John Tyler was a great uncle of which other President?

Extra. What President was related to eleven other Presidents, five by blood and six by marriage?

QUIZ 142: PRESIDENTS OF
FICTION—MOVIES _____

1. What former husband of actress Joan Crawford played the President of the United States in the 1962 movie *Advise and Consent?*

2. What comic actor played President Merken Muffley in the 1964 movie *Dr. Strangelove,* one of three roles he played in the film?

3. What actor played the young President Max Frost in the 1968 film, *Wild In the Streets,* in which eleven-year-olds were given the right to vote?

4. James Franciscus played President James Cassidy, who was based on John F. Kennedy, in what 1978 motion picture?

5. What comedian played President Manfred Link in the 1980 film *First Family?*

6. What actor played the President in the 1964 movie *Fail-Safe,* and again in the 1979 movie *Meteor?*

7. President Richard M. Monckton was played by what actor in the 1977 TV movie, *Washington: Behind Closed Doors?*

8. Actor E. G. Marshall played the President in what 1978 superhero movie?

9. The son of which western actor and singer played President Chet Roosevelt in the 1980 comedy film *Americathon?*

10. What British-born actor played the President who is captured by prisoners in the 1981 movie *Escape From New York?*

QUIZ 143: THE PRESS _____

1. Who was the first President to hold a press conference?

2. Who was the first President to grant an interview with a professional newsman, James Gordon Bennett?

3. What President was once the publisher of the *Marion Star* newspaper in Marion, Ohio?

4. Who was the first President ever to grant an interview to a Russian reporter of *Pravda?*

5. What was the title of First Lady Eleanor Roosevelt's newspaper column'?

6. What President was editor of the Harvard University school paper, the *Harvard Crimson?*

7. What President once beat up a newspaper editor for writing an article insulting his father?

8. As a young man what President worked as a writer for William Randolph Hearst's International News Service?

9. In 1948 what newspaper ran the erroneous but famous headline DEWEY DEFEATS TRUMAN?

10. What First Lady worked for the *Washington Times-Herald* as the Inquiring Camera Girl, and once interviewed Patricia Nixon?

11. What nickname for Richard Nixon did Southern California's *Independent Review* introduce to the American language in 1950?

12. What President wrote a daily newspaper column titled "Thinking Things Over With _____" about politics and government?

13. The founder of the *New York Tribune* was a candidate for President in 1872. Name him.

14. What newspaperman was once called an S.O.B. by President Harry S Truman?

15. Who were the two *Washington Post* journalists who uncovered the Watergate coverup?

QUIZ 144: PROGRAMS _____

Match the Presidents with their programs:

1. John F. Kennedy A. The Great Society

2. Franklin D. Roosevelt B. The New Deal

3. Theodore Roosevelt C. A New Beginning

4. Jimmy Carter D. New Frontier

5. Woodrow Wilson E. New Foundation

6. Lyndon Johnson F. Back to Normalcy

7. Harry S Truman G. The Square Deal

8. Warren G. Harding H. New Freedom

9. Dwight D. Eisenhower I. Peace and Prosperity

10. James Monroe J. The Era of Good Feeling

11. Ronald Reagan K. Fair Deal

QUIZ 145: PROTECTION _____

1. The Secret Service convinced what First Lady to carry a pistol in her purse after her life had been threatened?

2. What was the the name of the drunken guard who was supposed to have protected President Abraham Lincoln at Ford's Theatre but wandered off instead?

3. What detective protected Abraham Lincoln during his inaugural trip to Washington, D.C., in 1861?

4. Congress authorized the Secret Service to protect the President after the assassination of which President?

5. The Secret Service began to protect the Vice President of the United States in what year?

Extra. What widow and former First Lady was the first to be protected by the Secret Service for the rest of her life?

Extra. How many Secret Service agents were at the 1984 wedding of President Ronald Reagan's and First Lady Nancy Reagan's daughter Patty Davis to Paul Grilley, which was attended by 130 guests?

QUIZ 146: QUOTATIONS ABOUT PRESIDENTS _____

1. Who first conferred the title of Father of his Country on George Washington?

2. Who referred to George Washington as "First in war, first in peace, first in the hearts of his countrymen"?

3. To whom was Secretary of War Edwin M. Stanton referring when he said "Now he belongs to the ages"?

4. In 1901 to whom was Senator Mark Hanna of Ohio referring when he uttered the immortal words, "Now look! That damned cowboy is President of the United States"?

5. What President's Attorney General once said of him, "He tells so many lies that he convinces himself after a while he's telling the truth. He just doesn't recognize truth or falsehood"?

QUIZ 147: QUOTATIONS ABOUT THE WHITE HOUSE _____

Match the quotation about the White House with the person who said it:

1. "I would rather be a doorkeeper in the house of God then live in that palace at Washington."

A. Harry S Truman

2. "Nobody lives in the White House, they just come and go."

B. William Howard Taft

3. "A bully pulpit."

C. Calvin Coolidge

4. "The great white jail on Pennsylvania Avenue."

D. Theodore Roosevelt

5. "The loneliest place in the world."

E. First Lady Rachel Donelson

QUIZ 148: QUOTATIONS BY PRESIDENTS _____

Name the Presidents who have spoken the following words:

1. "My fellow Americans, ask not what your country can do for you—ask what you can do for your country."

2. "Speak softly, but carry a big stick."

3. "The business of America is business."

4. "I'm not smart enough to lie."

5. "After eight years as President, I have only two regrets: that I have not shot Henry Clay or hanged John C. Calhoun."

6. "A house divided against itself cannot stand."

7. "As to the Presidency, the two happiest days of my life were those of my entrance upon the office and my surrender of it."

8. "I shall go to Korea."

9. "Okay, let's get this plane back to Washington."

10. "Ripping, simply ripping."

QUIZ 149: QUOTATIONS FROM ONE PRESIDENT ABOUT ANOTHER PRESIDENT _____

1. About which future President was Harry S Truman speaking when he said, "_____ is a no-good lying bastard. He can lie out of both sides of his mouth at the same time, and if he ever caught himself telling the truth, he'd lie just to keep his hand in."

2. Who said the following about George Washington: "The President is fortunate to get off just as the bubble is bursting, leaving others to hold the bag"?

3. John F. Kennedy once remarked, "I think this is the most extraordinary collection of talent, of human knowledge, that has ever been gathered together in the White House, with the possible exception of when _____ dined alone."

4. What President said, "The principles of Jefferson are the axioms of a free society"?

5. Thomas Jefferson referred to which President as the Atlas of American Independence?

QUIZ 150: RADIO _____

1. Who was the first President to speak over the radio?

2. Early in his career, Ronald Reagan broadcast from Davenport, Iowa, on WOC radio. What do the call letters WOC stand for?

3. Who became the first President to broadcast from a foreign country, Cartagena, Columbia?

4. What President addressed the French people over the radio on November 2, 1942, and was thus the first President to speak on the air in a foreign language?

5. Which President's inauguration was the first to be described over the radio?

6. Who was the first President to have his voice broadcast via satellite?

7. Ronald Reagan was a sports broadcaster for what Des Moines, Iowa, radio station in the 1930s?

8. What President made the following joke just five minutes before his weekly radio broadcast: "My fellow Americans, I am pleased to announce I just signed legislation that will outlaw Russia forever. We begin bombing in five minutes"?

9. Ronald Reagan played disc jockey Andy McLeod in his 1937 movie debut for First National Pictures. What was the name of the film?

10. Ronald Reagan's second movie appearance was a small role as a radio announcer in what 1937 movie based on radio series gossip columnist Louella Parsons?

QUIZ 151: RAILROADS _____

1. Who was the first President to travel on a railroad train from Ellicott's Mills to Baltimore?

2. The son (Bernie) of which President was killed in a railroad accident on January 6, 1853, shortly after the President was sworn into office?

3. What President traveled 12,960 miles via the railroad over a six-week period in 1911?

4. Who was the first President to ride on a diesel-powered train in a trip between Washington, D.C. and New York City?

5. What President was shot and killed by Charles Guiteau as he was waiting for a train in the Washington train depot?

6. Who saved Robert Lincoln from death after he had fallen between two railroad cars at the Washington, D.C., railroad station?

7. What President campaigned across the country in 1948 in a Pullman train car named *Ferdinand Magellan?*

8. What President worked as a timekeeper for the Sante Fe Railroad?

9. What President was the son of a vice president of a railroad?

10. What name was given to the special chartered train that brought citizens of Plains, Georgia, to Washington, D.C., for Jimmy Carter's inauguration?

11. Which President's funeral train traveled 1,662 miles from Washington, D.C., to his place of burial in Springfield, Illinois?

12. Who was the first President to arrive in Washington, D.C., by train for his inauguration?

13. On January 14, 1893, what President was stricken by a heart attack while on board a train returning to Fremont, Ohio?

14. The son of which President was the president of the Pullman Company?

15. Who was the first President to depart Washington, D.C., by train after completing his term of office?

QUIZ 152: RE-ELECTIONS _____

1. Name the five Presidents whose last names began with the letter H who were not re-elected.

2. What amendment to the Constitution states that Presidents are limited to two full terms of office?

3. What President attempted to return to the White House in 1848 on the Free Soil Party ticket?

4. When Dwight D. Eisenhower ran for re-election, he offered Vice President Richard Nixon any cabinet post but one if he would step down as his running mate. What post wouldn't he offer Nixon?

5. Prior to President Franklin D. Roosevelt, who were the only two Presidents to try for a third term only to be defeated, one in the primary, the other in the election?

6. Who was the first President to serve a full term of office yet not seek re-election to a second term?

7. Who was the first President defeated for re-election?

8. How many Presidents have sought but failed to win renomination?

9. What President announced in his only inaugural speech that he would not be a candidate for re-election?

10. Who was the only President not renominated for re-election by his own party for a second term?

Extra. Only two Presidents ran unopposed for their second term of office; the first was George Washington, who was the second?

QUIZ 153: RELATIVES _____

1. What President was the third cousin twice removed of Robert E. Lee?

2. Supreme Court Chief Justice John Marshall was the second cousin once removed of which President?

3. Name the President who beat out his cousin Samuel for the Presidency.

4. Of which two Presidents was actor Wendell Corey a direct descendant?

5. Name the Academy Award–winning actor (1918–81) who was the second cousin of President Warren G. Harding.

6. Mormon leader Brigham Young was the fifth cousin once removed of which President?

7. What President was the ninth cousin of Leka I, the exiled King of Albania?

8. What President was a seventh cousin once removed of Prime Minister Winston Churchill?

9. Sarah Childress, who married President James Knox Polk, was which relative of President Andrew Jackson?

10. Author Ralph Waldo Emerson was a distant relative of what President?

QUIZ 154: RELIGION _____

1. Some people hid their Bibles in fear of having them taken away when who was elected President?

2. What President was baptized by a Methodist minister one week before his death on June 15, 1849?

3. What President was a minister of the Disciples of Christ?

4. Name the two Presidents who were both members of the Quaker religion.

5. Nine Presidents have been members of what religious denomination?

6. Eleven Vice Presidents have been members of what religious denomination?

7. How many President and Vice President teams have both been of the same religious persuasion?

8. Who was the first Catholic elected President?

9. What President annually read the Bible from cover to cover?

QUIZ 155: RETREATS _____

1. Where was President Franklin D. Roosevelt's "Little White House" located?

2. What name did President Franklin D. Roosevelt give the Presidential retreat located in the Maryland Hills?

3. What new name did President Dwight D. Eisenhower give Shangri-La in 1953?

4. At what Washington, D.C., location did President Abraham Lincoln enjoy spending time away from the White House where he composed the final draft of his Emancipation Proclamation in 1862?

5. Where was President Richard M. Nixon's "Western White House" located?

QUIZ 156: ROMANCES _____

1. The father of which President was rumored to have been romantically involved with actress Gloria Swanson?

2. What President was rejected by three women before a widow finally accepted his marriage proposal?

3. What President carried on a romance with Sally Hemings, one of his 130 slaves?

4. What President was romantically involved with a young lady named Ann Rutledge who died of malaria at the age of twenty-two?

5. What was the name of the British driver romantically linked to General Dwight D. Eisenhower during World War II?

6. First Lady Eleanor Roosevelt was not happy when she discovered that her husband, President Franklin D. Roosevelt, had been seeing what woman in Warm Springs, Georgia?

7. What President had an affair with Nan Britton while he was in the White House, making love in a twenty-five-square-foot closet near the Oval Office?

8. What President was romantically linked with actress Marilyn Monroe?

9. What President once dated Academy Award–winning actress Patricia Neal?

10. Model Phyllis Brown was once the love interest of which President?

QUIZ 157: RUNNING MATES _____

1. Who was the running mate on the Equal Rights ticket of Presidential candidate Victoria Woodhull in 1872?

2. Who was the first woman running mate for the Presidency endorsed by a major political party?

3. Name the former U.S. Army general who was Barry Goldwater's Vice Presidential running mate in 1964.

4. In 1972 Presidential candidate George McGovern said he was "1000 percent behind" his running mate until it was revealed that the Vice Presidential candidate once spent time in a hospital for severe mental depression. Who was he?

5. Who were Adlai Stevenson's running mates in 1952 and 1956?

QUIZ 158: SCANDALS _____

1. The infamous Teapot Dome scandal occurred during which President's administration?

2. What President was considered to be an alcoholic, which eventually lead to his death?

3. What bachelor President was rumored to have had a homosexual relationship with his Vice President, William Rufus King?

4. As governor of Virginia what President was accused of cowardice when he fled during a British attack?

5. Although three Presidents have been accused of fathering illegitimate children, who was the only President to admit that he actually had?

6. What Presidential candidate was charged with having branded his initials on the shoulders of forty-three slaves?

7. What President was suspected of voting fraud in his election to the Senate that won him the nickname of "Landslide _____"?

8. What Vice President who later became President was accused of accepting a substantial sum of money from business interests to assist his political career?

9. What bachelor Vice President was dropped from renomination when it was revealed that he had fathered two daughters?

10. While still a soldier, what President was threatened with a court-martial because of his heavy drinking?

Extra. What President was embroiled in the Irangate affair?

QUIZ 159: SCHOOLING _____

1. What President was taught to read, write, and figure math by his wife Eliza?

2. What President graduated from a Texas high school that bore his last name?

3. What President attempted to enroll in the U.S. Naval Academy at Annapolis but found that he was over the age limit?

4. What President attempted to enroll in the U.S. Military Academy at West Point but was turned down because he had poor eyesight?

5. Who was the first President to graduate from prep school when he graduated from Groton?

6. What President attended public school in Germany?

7. President John F. Kennedy and singer Mick Jagger both attended what same school in London?

8. What President invited two prostitutes to a school dance, expecting them not to show up, but they did?

9. What President was married to a teacher of the deaf (Grace)?

10. What President was an assistant teacher of the blind in New York City?

QUIZ 160: SECONDS ────────────

1. George Washington gave the shortest inaugural address in history; who gave the second shortest?

2. President William Henry Harrison served just thirty-two days, the shortest term of office of any President; who served the second shortest term of 199 days?

3. William Rufus King, who died before he could be sworn in, served the shortest term of office as Vice President; who served the second shortest term as Vice President?

4. John Adams lived the longest of any President, dying at the age of 90 years and 247 days; who lived the second longest, 90 years and 71 days?

5. Franklin D. Roosevelt was the first Democratic President to die in office; who was the second?

Extra. In 1900 George Washington was the first President inducted into New York University's Hall of Fame of Great Americans. Who was the second President inducted?

Extra. John C. Calhoun became the first Vice President to resign his office. Who was the second?

QUIZ 161: SECRETARY OF STATE _____

1. What President served as President Thomas Jefferson's Secretary of State?

2. What President served as the Secretary of State and Secretary of War under President James Madison?

3. Who served as President James Monroe's Secretary of State and negotiated the purchase of Florida from Spain?

4. William Jennings Bryan served as Secretary of State to which President?

5. Dean Acheson served as Secretary of State to which President?

6. Secretary of State William H. Seward purchased Alaska for the United States at a cost of $7.2 million dollars. What President did he represent?

7. Who was President Theodore Roosevelt's Nobel Peace Prize–winning Secretary of State?

8. What President had a Secretary of State named John Forsyth?

9. How many Presidents have previously served as Secretaries of State?

10. Name the only President to serve as Secretary of State on two occasions.

11. John Watson Foster served as President Benjamin Harrison's Secretary of State. Under which President did his grandson, John Foster Dulles, serve as Secretary of State?

12. What Secretary of State served the longest length of office, a record twelve years with Presidents Franklin D. Roosevelt and Harry S Truman?

13. Who was President John Tyler's Secretary of State, killed on board the *Princeton* when its Peacemaker cannon exploded?

14. Name the former U.S. Army general who became Secretary of State

under President Harry S Truman, and in 1953 was awarded the Nobel Peace Prize.

15. Name President Harry S Truman's fourth Secretary of State, whose memoirs, *Present at the Creation,* won him a Pulitzer Prize.

QUIZ 162: SECRETARY OF WAR _____

1. The father (Alphonso) of which President served as President Ulysses S. Grant's Secretary of War?

2. Impeachment proceedings were brought against President Andrew Johnson after he dismissed what Secretary of War?

3. President Chester A. Arthur's Secretary of War was the son of which previous President?

4. Who served as President Franklin Pierce's Secretary of War?

5. What former Vice President served as Secretary of War for the Confederacy?

Extra. What Secretary of War under President James Buchanan resigned to become a brigadier general in the Confederacy?

Extra. What trophy did President Calvin Coolidge's Secretary of War Dwight F. Davis introduce to sports?

QUIZ 163: SECRET SERVICE CODE NAMES _____

Match the person with the Secret Service code name:

1. Nelson Rockefeller   A. Lancer

2. Betty Ford   B. Rawhide

3. Lyndon Johnson   C. Sandstorm

4. Ronald Reagan   D. Passkey

5. Bess Truman   E. Volunteer

6. John F. Kennedy   F. Rainbow

7. Lady Bird Johnson   G. Lace

8. Gerald Ford   H. Victoria

9. Jacqueline Kennedy   I. Fernlake

10. Nancy Reagan   J. Pinafore

QUIZ 164: THE SENATE _____

1. What President resigned from the U.S. Senate in 1842 because his wife, Jane, hated living in Washington, D.C.?

2. Who was the only President to serve as a senator after having served as President?

3. In 1813 what future senator shot a future President?

4. Name the President who won his Senate seat by defeating the grandson of the man who defeated his grandfather for the Senate in 1916.

5. At this President's birth on August 27, 1908, his father bragged prophetically that "A United States senator was born this morning." Name the President.

6. Who was the first President elected to office while he was serving in the U.S. Senate?

7. Who was the first Vice President elected by the Senate?

8. Who was the first President who served as a senator?

9. What former First Lady was voted a seat in the U.S. Senate?

10. How many Vice Presidents returned to the Senate after serving as Vice President?

11. In 1832 who resigned his office of Vice President to become a senator?

12. How many Presidents served both as a representative and a senator?

13. Name the only two men to go directly from the U.S. Senate to the Presidency.

14. Who was the only President elected to the U.S. Senate who didn't serve because he had also been elected to the Presidency?

15. What is the greatest number of votes that can occur in the U.S. Senate?

QUIZ 165: SISTERS ⎯⎯⎯⎯⎯⎯⎯⎯⎯⎯⎯⎯

1. What President had a retarded sister, Elizabeth, who died at the age of thirty?

2. The sister of which President wrote a best-selling book entitled *The Gift of Inner Healing?*

3. The sister of which President underwent a prefrontal lobotomy operation when she was twenty-one years old?

4. The sister (Corinne) of which President founded the first Red Cross War Chapter?

5. What President was the brother of twin siblings, a girl and a boy?

QUIZ 166: SLAVERY _____

1. What happened to the part of the Declaration of Independence in which Thomas Jefferson condemned slavery?

2. What document did President Abraham Lincoln issue on January 1, 1863, giving freedom to the three million slaves in the South?

3. How many Presidents of the United States were slave owners?

4. What President signed a bill that forbade slavery within the District of Columbia?

5. A group of former slaves returned to Africa to establish a country named Liberia and named their capital city after what U.S. President?

6. By 1861 what were the only three countries in the western world to allow slavery?

7. What President signed into law a bill that banned the importation of slaves?

8. What President owned a slave named Hercules who served as his White House cook?

9. What President put down a slave revolt while he was governor of Virginia?

10. Who urged the Confederacy to purchase forty thousand slaves, draft them into the Confederate Army, and free them after the Civil War was concluded?

Extra. What President defended slaves in court and once helped six slaves to obtain their freedom?

QUIZ 167: SONS _____

1. The twenty-eight-year-old son of which President committed suicide in 1829 when he jumped off a New York–bound ship?

2. What President lost three of his four sons to World War I and World War II?

3. What President saw his son killed in a railroad accident just two months prior to his inauguration?

4. What President had a son who danced with the Joffrey Ballet Company in New York?

5. What was the most popular name among the sons of the Presidents?

6. What President had five sons who served in the Confederacy during the Civil War?

7. Only once did government offices close upon the death of a son of a President. Which President's son received such an honor?

8. The son of which President sometimes accompanied his father into battle, even though he was just a boy?

9. The son (Quentin) of which President was killed in battle during World War I, the only son of a President to die in battle?

10. The Congressional Medal of Honor was awarded to which two sons of Presidents?

11. Which President's only son, Richard, served as a general with the Confederacy during the Civil War?

12. The adopted son of which President raced speedboats for a hobby and won one world championship in 1967?

13. The sons of two Presidents were graduates of West Point. Who were they?

14. The son of which President was asked to run for the Presidency by the Whig Party in 1856, but turned it down?

15. The son of which President turned down an offer to run for the Presidency in 1848 on the Free Soil Ticket? (His father accepted the nomination instead but lost to Zachary Taylor.)

QUIZ 168: SPEECHES _____

1. What President made some of his campaign speeches in German?

2. What President gave a total of twenty-seven fireside chats over a six-year period?

3. Name the President who coined the expression "rugged individualism."

4. Only two non-Brittons have addressed a joint session of the British Parliament—French President Charles De Gaulle and what U.S. President?

5. What President earned the nickname Napoleon of the Stumps because of his sarcastic speeches?

6. What President spoke 985 words without once uttering the word "I" during his inaugural speech?

7. On March 4, 1853, who was the first President to deliver his inaugural address from notes instead of reading it?

8. What President's speech is read in Congress each year?

9. What President suffered a paralytic stroke while giving a speech in Pueblo, Colorado, which affected him for the rest of his life?

10. What were the four freedoms to which President Franklin D. Roosevelt referred in his famous inaugural address?

Extra. Who was the first President to make a speech from the White House via telecast?

Extra. Name the President who gave a fifty-minute speech after being shot and wounded by John F. Schrank in Milwaukee, Wisconsin.

QUIZ 169: SPORTS _____

1. What President turned on the lights for the first major league baseball game at night at Crosley Field in Cincinnati?

2. Who was the first President to take up the sport of golf?

3. During his film career Ronald Reagan portrayed what two real-life athletes? Name both films.

4. Name the two Presidents who shot holes-in-one in golf.

5. Who was the first President to throw out a baseball to open the baseball season?

6. What President spent a few rounds in the ring with heavyweight boxing champion John L. Sullivan?

7. What First Lady was a champion shot-putter and basketball player in high school?

8. What President was playing baseball when he was informed that he had been nominated as the Republican candidate for President?

9. While a student at Yale, what President was a member of the Yale rowing team?

10. What President was such an ardent golfer that he played with black golf balls in the Washington snow?

11. What President could throw out the opening day baseball with either hand?

12. In what city did Ronald Reagan throw out the ceremonial opening day baseball in 1984?

13. What President played outfield for his college baseball team?

14. What President liked to boast that he had a larger chest expansion than heavyweight boxer Jack Dempsey?

15. What President was the first Chief Executive to throw out a baseball to open a World Series?

QUIZ 170: STATES _____

1. Name the four state capitals named for Presidents.

2. More Vice Presidents have come from what state than any other?

3. What President was the first President of all fifty states?

4. Who was the first President to visit all fifty states while in office?

5. What state is called the Mother of Presidents because it has produced eight Presidents?

6. What state was originally incorporated under the name of Jefferson after Thomas Jefferson?

7. What two Presidents were born in Texas?

8. On August 22, 1853, what Illinois town named itself after a man who would one day be elected President?

9. During George Washington's two terms of office what three new states were admitted to the original thirteen?

10. What state holds the first Presidential primary?

Extra. Name the only state capital named after a President before he was elected.

Extra. More states were admitted to the Union during which President's administration than any other?

Extra. Who was the first Democratic President to carry the state of Vermont?

QUIZ 171: STATUES _____

1. Charles Bulfinch was the sculptor of what statue of a naked President?

2. A statue of which American President stands in Trafalgar Square in London, England?

3. From 1847 until 1874 a statue of which President stood on the White House lawn—the only monument to a President on the White House grounds?

4. What President was the subject of the first equestrian statue erected in the United States?

5. What four Presidents have statues in the Hall of Fame in the Capitol in Washington, D.C.?

Extra. General Winfield Scott and what President each have two equestrian statues in Washington, D.C.?

Extra. The newspaper boys of America pitched in their pennies to have the statue of a President's pet dog made and put on display at the Smithsonian Institution. Name that dog.

QUIZ 172: STRIKES _____

1. What President helped lead a strike against the college administration at Eureka College?

2. As president of the Screen Actors Guild what President lead a strike against the movie studios?

3. What President fired members of PATCO because they struck for better pay and working conditions in August 1981?

4. Railroad workers staged the first national strike in 1877 while who was serving as President?

5. What President in 1894 called out federal troops during the Pullman strike stating "If it takes the entire Army and Navy of the United States to deliver a postcard in Chicago, that card will be delivered"?

Extra. What President as governor of Massachusetts broke the Boston police strike, stating that "there is no right to strike against the public safety by anybody, anywhere, any time"?

QUIZ 173: SUPREME COURT —————

1. Who was the only President to sit on the Supreme Court where he served as Chief Justice from 1921 until 1930?

2. Who was the first President to be administered the oath of office by a justice of the Supreme Court?

3. What President served as a Superior Court Justice in the state of Tennessee?

4. What was the name of the woman whom President Ronald Reagan appointed to the Supreme Court in July 1981?

5. What President won his case defending the Illinois Central Railroad before the Supreme Court?

6. John Adams's last act as President was to appoint which man as the Chief Justice of the Supreme Court?

7. What former all-American football player was appointed to the Supreme Court by President John F. Kennedy?

8. Who did President Dwight D. Eisenhower appoint in 1953 to replace Chief Justice Fred Vinson on the Supreme Court?

9. Who was the only President to appoint four Chief Justices?

10. Name Franklin D. Roosevelt's first appointee to the Supreme Court who was at one time associated with the Ku Klux Klan.

11. What President argued and lost two cases before the Supreme Court?

12. During which President's administration was the tenth seat on the Supreme Court abolished?

13. Name the President who appointed Bushrod Washington, the nephew of George Washington, to the Supreme Court.

14. Who was the first and only President to address the Supreme Court while in office?

15. What President unsuccessfully attempted to increase the number of justices on the Supreme Court to fifteen so that he could select the additional six members?

QUIZ 174: TEACHERS _____

1. What President taught school for several years although he never attended college?

2. What President taught both Greek and Latin at Hiram College in Ohio?

3. Prior to becoming president of Princeton, what President taught history at three different colleges?

4. What President was a schoolteacher as well as the son of schoolteachers?

5. Upon graduating Phi Beta Kappa from Union College, what President became a schoolteacher in Vermont?

6. While serving as President, who taught Sunday School on several occasions at the First Baptist Church in Washington?

7. What President at the age of sixteen was an assistant teacher in an asylum for the blind?

8. What President's first job was to teach Latin in a one-room schoolhouse in Worcester, Massacusetts?

9. After scrving as the twenty-seventh President, who went on to become a law professor at Yale?

10. What President taught a men's Bible class at a Presbyterian church?

QUIZ 175: TELEPHONE _____

1. Who was the first President to use the telephone for campaign purposes?

2. What President addressed the opening session of the United Nations in San Francisco by telephone?

3. Name the first President to be interviewed over the telephone.

4. Who was President when the first telephone was installed in the White House?

5. Who was the first President to use the Hot Line between the White House and Moscow?

QUIZ 176: TELEVISION _____

1. Who was the first President to appear on nonpublic television on WNBT at the opening of the New York World's Fair?

2. Who was the first President to appear on national television in a news conference?

3. The son (Steven) of which President appeared on the TV series "The Young and the Restless", playing the role of Andy Richards?

4. Who were the first Presidential candidates to debate each other on television?

5. Who was the first President to be televised from the White House?

6. Who was the first President to appear on television in color?

7. What President held the first live TV press conference?

8. What President appeared on TV's "What's My Line?" during his tenure as governor?

9. What President asked the question "Sock it to me?" on TV's "Laugh-In"?

10. What President's inauguration was the first to be televised using hand signals for the deaf?

11. Before becoming President, who appeared as a mystery guest on the TV game show "What's My Line?" in August 1969?

12. Who was the only President to own interest in both radio and television stations?

13. Who was the first President to address the Russian people on Soviet television?

14. Where and in what year were political party national conventions first televised?

15. What First Lady hosted a two-part PBS TV program entitled "The Chemical People"?

16. First Lady Betty Ford made a cameo appearance on what popular TV sitcom?

17. Who were the hosts of the television program "The Ev and Jerry Show"?

18. Who appeared on television to tell the American people, "I'm no crook"?

19. What First Lady was addicted to television soap operas?

20. Who was the only First Lady to win an Emmy for a TV special in which she hosted a tour of the White House?

QUIZ 177: TERMS OF OFFICE _____

1. The Era of Good Feeling was the nickname given to the two terms of office of which President?

2. What President served the shortest term of office, just thirty days, before he died prematurely?

3. What effect did the passage of the Twenty-second Amendment to the Constitution in 1951 have on Presidential tenure?

4. What President's term of office has been referred to as the Imperial Presidency?

5. What President served a full term of office, yet it was less than four years?

QUIZ 178: TRADITIONS _____

1. What President began the tradition of command performances when he asked opera singer Adelina Patti to sing at the White House?

2. What White House couple introduced the annual tradition of Easter Egg rolling on the White House lawn?

3. What President started a tradition when he threw out the ball to open the baseball season?

4. What President threw out the ten millionth Spaulding baseball used in a major league baseball game?

5. First Lady Caroline Scott Harrison, wife of President Benjamin Harrison, began what annual White House tradition?

Extra. What First Lady began the tradition of using special White House china?

Extra. What President established the tradition of "executive privilege" when he refused to testify at Vice President Aaron Burr's trial for treason?

QUIZ 179: TRAVEL _____

1. What President was the first Chief Executive to travel in a submarine?

2. Who was the first President to visit foreign soil while in office when he went to Mexico to meet President Porforio Diaz?

3. Who was the first President to visit a U.S. Protectorate outside the continental United States when he visited Panama?

4. Who was the first President to travel to Europe while in office?

5. Who became the first President to leave the United States during wartime when he traveled to Africa?

6. Who was the first President to visit Moscow, the capital of the Soviet Union?

7. What President visited a record twenty-eight foreign countries while in office?

8. Who was the first President to visit the West Coast while in office when he attended a reunion of his old Ohio regiment?

9. At the age of fourteen, what future President traveled to Russia as the secretary to an envoy?

10. George Washington left the shores of America only once during his lifetime, when he traveled with his brother to which of the following islands?
    A. Azores
    B. Barbados
    C. Canary Islands
    D. Florida Keys

QUIZ 180: TREATIES _____

1. What President negotiated the treaty with Britain to end the Revolutionary War?

2. What President, one of three American commissioners, negotiated the treaty with Britain to end the War of 1812?

3. According to the Constitution, the President can make a treaty with another power subject to the approval of what body?

4. What President ended the United States' treaty with Taiwan in order to establish diplomatic relations with mainland China?

5. What President wrote the first trade treaty between the United States and Russia while he was serving as minister to Russia?

QUIZ 181: TRIOS _____

1. Name the three Presidents who were left-handed.

2. What three Presidents had red hair?

3. What three men served as President in 1841?

4. Name the three Presidents who died on the Fourth of July.

5. What three Presidents were born in Norfolk County, Massachusetts?

6. Name the only three Presidents who moved directly from the Vice Presidency to the Presidency by election.

7. Name President Franklin D. Roosevelt's three Vice Presidents.

8. Who were the only three consecutive Presidents to wear beards?

9. In 1881 the United States had three Presidents; who were they?

10. Name the three Presidents who were of Dutch ancestry.

QUIZ 182: TRUE OR FALSE _____

Are these statements true or false?

1. George Washington had wooden teeth.

2. George Washington threw a silver dollar across the Potomac.

3. Cleveland, Ohio, was named for President Grover Cleveland.

4. Madison, Wisconsin, was named for President James Madison.

5. Theodore Roosevelt was the youngest man to be elected President.

6. Singer Frank Sinatra named his son Frank Sinatra, Jr., after President Franklin D. Roosevelt.

7. President Ronald Reagan appeared in the 1952 movie *Bonzo Goes to College*.

8. There were wives of Presidents who were not First Ladies.

9. No American President has ever lost an election during wartime.

10. Abraham Lincoln once wrote a letter to Horace Greeley stating, "If I could save the Union without freeing any slave I would do it."

Extra. The actual building in which George Washington was born can be toured for an admission price.

QUIZ 183: VETOES _____

1. What Vice President resigned his office because President Andrew Jackson vetoed a bill to renew the charter of the Bank of the United States?

2. During President Andrew Jackson's two terms of office he vetoed how many bills, none of which were overridden by Congress?

3. What President was nicknamed Old Veto because he vetoed so many bills from Congress?

4. During what President's combined terms of office did he veto eighty-two bills with only one overridden by Congress?

5. What President used the veto a record 631 times during his terms of office?

6. The first veto in United States history was made by President George Washington during his second term. What was the subject of the bill?

7. What President holds the distinction of having had the most vetoes overriden by Congress, fifteen out of twenty-eight?

8. If the President doesn't veto a bill after its passage, in how many days does it automatically become law?

9. What President defended the veto calling it "a breakwater, to arrest or suspend for a time being hasty and improvident legislation until the people have time and opportunity to consider its propriety"?

10. What President was the first to use the pocket veto?

11. Congress granted blacks the right to vote in Washington, D.C., over the veto of which President?

12. Who was nicknamed the Veto President when he became the first President to veto one hundred bills?

13. Who was the first President to have a veto overridden by Congress?

14. Who was the first of eight Presidents never to use the veto power?

15. What President had the second highest number of vetoes during his two terms of office?

QUIZ 184: VICE PRESIDENTS _____

1. Who was the only Vice President to serve two full terms as President?

2. Who was the first Vice President to resign from office (three months prior to the end of his term)?

3. Who was the first Vice President to succeed to the Presidency upon the death of a President?

4. What President turned down Ronald Reagan's offer to run as his Vice President in 1980?

5. Secretary of the Treasury Alexander Hamilton was shot and killed in a duel with which Vice President?

6. Alben Barkley, the oldest Vice President, served under which President?

7. Who was the first Vice President to succeed to the Presidency and then win the office at the next election?

8. Who was the only Vice President to take the oath of office outside of the United States?

9. Who was the only President who, when he was the Vice President, did not succeed the President he served under?

10. Who was the only President to run for office without a Vice Presidential running mate?

11. Who was the first Vice President to hold the position of Deputy President Pro Tempore of the Senate?

12. Who was the only Vice President to serve as a representative from North Carolina and a senator from Alabama?

13. Only two Vice Presidents served under two different Presidents. Name them and the Presidents under whom they served.

14. What President had two Vice Presidents die in office?

15. Who served as Vice President for only one month before serving as President?

16. What single duty does the Constitution give the Vice President?

17. Which one of President Franklin D. Roosevelt's three Vice Presidents described the Vice President's job as "not worth a pitcher of warm spit"?

18. What is the most common last name for a Vice President?

19. Name the only two Vice Presidents who have been elected to the Presidency twice.

QUIZ 185: WARS _____

1. What war was termed "Mr. Madison's War" and "Mr. Madison's Ruinous War"?

2. What President held the position of U.S. Commander of European Theater Operations during World War II?

3. What President commanded the American forces at the Battle of New Orleans during the War of 1812?

4. Who served as President during the Korean War?

5. Who was President when the Spanish-American War broke out?

6. What two men served as President during the Vietnam War?

7. Who was the only President to fight in three wars: the War of 1812, the Black Hawk War, and the Mexican War?

8. In October 1891 President Benjamin Harrison asked Congress for a declaration of war against what South American country after two U.S. sailors were killed?

9. Who was President when the United States fought the Barbary pirates in the Tripolitan War?

10. What President on horesback led his Rough Riders on foot up San Juan Hill during "that splendid little war" with Spain?

11. Who became the first President to take office during wartime?

12. What President and his brother were taken prisoner by the British during the Revolutionary War?

13. What young Congressman from Illinois demanded that President James Knox Polk show the exact spot on American soil where Mexican soldiers allegedly crossed onto American soil and killed Americans, thus beginning the Mexican War?

14. During what war did President James A. Garfield receive several bullet wounds?

15. Name the six Presidents who were in the service during World War II.

16. During what war was John F. Kennedy born?

17. What President defended Fort Harrison against the Indian chief, Tecumseh, in 1812, and later fought off an attack by the Mexican general Santa Anna in the Mexican War?

18. During which war did President Harry S Truman serve?

19. The White House was burned by the British during which war?

20. What President asked Congress for a declaration of war after the United States had been attacked at Pearl Harbor?

QUIZ 186: WEAPONS _____

1. What President was shot with a Roehm RG-14 .22-caliber pistol outside the Washington Hilton?

2. What were the names of the two pistols that Franklin and Eleanor Roosevelt kept under their pillows at night?

3. Who was the only President to authorize the use of atomic weapons during wartime?

4. Charles J. Guiteau shot and killed what President with a .44 English bulldog pistol?

5. After the assassination attempt on President Andrew Jackson's life in 1835, which senator, who later became President, began carrying two pistols even into the Senate chamber?

Extra. What assassin purchased a 6.5mm Nanulicher Carcano high-powered rifle under the name of A. Hidell?

Extra. What assassin used a single shot .44 derringer to do his dirty deed?

QUIZ 187: WEDDINGS _____

1. On March 17, 1905, what President gave the bride away at her wedding to a man who would one day be President?

2. Who became the first President to marry in the White House when he wed Frances Folson?

3. Who was the first President married while serving as Chief Executive?

4. What Academy Award winning–actor served as best man at the wedding of Ronald Reagan to Nancy Davis on January 26, 1940?

5. Who was the only son of a President to get married in the White House?

6. Who was married on June 12, 1971, at the only White House wedding held outside on the grounds?

7. The son of which President served as his father's best man when his father married twenty-two-year-old Letitia Christian?

8. Name the four Presidents who celebrated their golden wedding anniversaries.

9. How many daughters of Presidents have been married in the White House?

10. The daughter of which President married Secretary of the Treasury William Gibbs McAdoo in the White House on May 7, 1914?

QUIZ 188: WHITE HOUSE _____

1. Who was the first President to live in the White House?

2. When Calvin Coolidge made the first radio broadcast from the White House on February 22, 1914, what was the occasion?

3. Name the two Presidents who died in the White House.

4. Name the first President to be inaugurated into office in the White House.

5. What President had twenty-four wagonloads of furniture from the White House auctioned off before he and his family moved in?

6. Who was the first President to officially refer to the Executive Mansion as the White House?

7. Name the First Lady whose family's estate was nicknamed the White House.

8. For what 1942 movie were Ronald Reagan and Ann Sheridan originally considered for the lead roles?

9. What President on his last day of office in the White House, told his staff, "Take good care of this place, we'll be back"?

10. What President had a balcony added onto the White House that required the federal mint to change the design of the White House on the back of the $20 bill?

QUIZ 189: WITNESSES _____

1. What President's First Lady watched President Abraham Lincoln's funeral procession at the age of three?

2. What assassin witnessed the hanging of abolitionist John Brown on December 2, 1859?

3. The second wife of which President was present at the wedding of her husband to his first wife, Alice Hathaway Lee, in 1880?

4. What President and First Lady watched each other graduate from high school in 1901 since they were in the same class?

5. What President as an eight-year-old boy watched the Battle of Bunker Hill from his family's farm in Braintree?

QUIZ 190: WORDS AND PHRASES _____

1. What President was responsible for coining the word "muckrakers"?

2. What Vice President lent his last name to the word "gerrymandering"?

3. What was President Calvin Coolidge's reply to a young woman who told him that she made a bet that she could get him to say more than two words?

4. During a 1928 campaign speech, what President coined the phrase, "the American system of rugged individualism"?

5. What President coined such phrases as "my hat's in the ring" and "lunatic fringe"?

6. The word "spectation" was coined by which sports-loving President?

7. "Founding Fathers" was coined by which President?

8. Who coined the political slogan, "Don't swap horses while crossing a stream"?

9. The term "O.K." began as a slogan for which Presidential candidate?

10. What President gave the United Nations its name?

11. After whom was the poinsettia flower named?

12. The term "First Lady" was introduced during which President's administration?

13. Who was the first Vice President called "the Veep"?

14. "By the Eternal" was the favorite expletive of which President?

15. What President coined the phrase "good to the last drop," which Maxwell House Coffee adopted as their slogan?

16. What one word take-off on a President's name meant the saving of food and clothing during hard times?

17. What President coined the phrase "the ballot is stronger than the bullet"?

18. What President sent the famous Message to Garcia on the eve of the Spanish-American War?

19. The phrase "quality of life" was introduced by which Presidential candidate?

20. What former Vice President referred to journalists as "nattering nabobs of negativism"?

QUIZ 191: WORLD LEADERS _____

1. President Millard Fillmore was afraid that he might be requested to kiss the feet of which world leader upon meeting him?

2. What President met with German leader Adolf Hitler in Berlin?

3. Where did President Franklin D. Roosevelt meet for the first time with Soviet leader Joseph Stalin in November 1943?

4. With which world leader did Vice President Richard M. Nixon get into a shouting match while standing in a model American kitchen?

5. What President was a seventh cousin once removed of British Prime Minister Winston Churchill?

6. First Lady Elizabeth Monroe attended the coronation of which French ruler?

7. In 1940 what thirteen-year-old future Communist leader wrote to President Franklin D. Roosevelt asking him for $10, to which he received a reply but no money?

8. Vietnamese ruler Ho Chi Minh and what President were both born in 1890 and died in 1969?

9. What British Prime Minister has been suggested by some to have had a "crush" on an American President?

10. What President was greeted warmly by Chairman Mao Zedong when he visited China in February 1972?

QUIZ 192: WOUNDED _____

1. Who was the only President wounded during the Civil War (October 19, 1864, at the Battle of Cedar Creek)?

2. What President was wounded at Trenton during the American Revolution and carried the bullet in his body for the rest of his life?

3. What President gave a speech in Milwaukee on Ocober 14, 1912, just after he had been shot?

4. What President died from the doctor's probing of his wound and not from the bullet itself?

5. What Presidential Press Secretary was wounded during the attempted assassination of President Ronald Reagan?

6. What President carried a bullet in him for the rest of his life from a duel that he had with Charles Dickinson, whom he had shot and killed in 1806?

7. Thomas Hart Benton and his brother shot and wounded what President in Nashville in 1813?

8. Name the three Presidents who have been wounded in action during a war.

9. Name the only President wounded from an assassination attempt while in office.

10. What President as a young boy was cut by the saber of a British officer?

QUIZ 193: WRITING _____

1. What President as a boy made a list of one hundred rules for good etiquette?

2. What President was nicknamed the sage of his time?

3. Which President wrote for the *Boston Gazette* in 1766 under the pen name of Clarendon?

4. What President was employed as a sportswriter?

5. The signatures of which two Presidents are the most valuable?

6. In June 1930 what President's newspaper column, "Thinking Things Over With _____," was published in the *New York Herald Tribune?*

7. Columbus and Publicola were two pen names used by which President?

8. What President was ambidextrous, enabling him to simultaneously write Latin with one hand and Greek with the other?

9. What President wrote the most books of any Chief Executive?

10. What President wrote *The Happy Warrior, Alfred E. Smith,* which was published in 1928?

QUIZ 194: EXTRA #1 _____

1. In the 1950s what First Lady appeared in a magazine advertisement for Parkay margarine?

2. What historical key did Lafayette present to George Washington, which Washington kept at Mount Vernon?

3. What President was depicted on the last silver coin minted in the United States?

4. What President and his successor were both born in 1913?

5. What Vice President under William McKinley was called the Assistant President?

QUIZ 195: EXTRA #2 _____

1. What Vice President will always be remembered for one line that he spoke, "What this country needs is a good five-cent cigar"?

2. What President served as Vice President for two terms?

3. What movie did President Richard M. Nixon watch in the White House the night before he ordered the invasion of Cambodia?

4. What President's mother-in-law publicly stated that he would lose to his opponent during the Presidential election?

5. What President changed his name so that his initials would not read HUG?

QUIZ 196: EXTRA #3 _____

1. What President called Prohibition "the greatest noble experiment in history"?

2. Who was the only President to study medicine?

3. Spring Byington (in 1938) and Ginger Rogers (in 1946) both portrayed what First Lady on the silver screen?

4. What First Lady smoked a corncob pipe?

5. In 1887 and again in 1901 which President's coffin was opened to check if his body was still inside?

QUIZ 197: EXTRA #4 _____

1. Diarrhea was the official cause of death of which former President?

2. Prior to serving as President Franklin D. Roosevelt's Vice President during his third term of office, Henry A. Wallace served as the Secretary of what cabinet department?

3. Name the President who served as Secretary of War and Secretary of the Interior simultaneously during the War of 1812.

4. What three Presidents were middle children who became generals?

5. What President was the son of a Presbyterian minister?

QUIZ 198: EXTRA #5 _____

1. Al Stillman composed the lyrics, but what famous bandleader wrote the music for the song "Viva Roosevelt" (a conga-march)?

2. The admission to which President's birthplace at 24 North Coalter Street in Staunton, Virginia, costs one dollar?

3. Who was the only Vice President married while in office and also the last Vice President born in a log cabin?

4. Who were the only two Vice Presidents to serve under two different Presidents?

5. The Department of Justice was established under which President?

QUIZ 199: EXTRA #6 _____

1. What President dedicated the National Press Club in Washington, D.C., on February 4, 1928?

2. Name the two Presidents who became law professors.

3. In drawing up the Constitution what limit did the Founding Fathers set on how long a President could serve in office?

4. Name the only First Lady to die after her husband's election but just prior to his inauguration.

5. Who was the only man elected President with fewer electoral votes and fewer popular votes than his opponent?

QUIZ 200: TOUGH AND TRICKY QUESTIONS—THE FINAL TEST

1. Did President Abraham Lincoln see the entire play *Our American Cousin* from beginning to end before he was fatally shot?

2. Where did George Washington give his Farewell Address?

3. Millard Fillmore was born on January 7, 1800, in what century?

4. Who is buried in Grant's Tomb?

5. Who wrote the 1961 best-selling book *PT-109?*

6. What President twice refused a post on the Supreme Court?

7. What Presidential candidate and relative of a President used the slogan "We're ready for Teddy"?

8. What Presidential candidate worked as a newspaper boy for the *Marion Star* in Marion, Ohio?

9. The brother of which President was a Chief Justice?

10. Did Franklin D. Roosevelt ever serve as a Vice President?

11. What President lived in Poland for a while as a young boy?

12. According to the Twenty-second Amendment, adopted in 1951, what is the limit on how many terms of office a President can serve?

13. When Presidents Richard M. Nixon, Gerald Ford, and Jimmy Carter all traveled together on the Presidential aircraft to Cairo, Egypt, for Anwar Sadat's funeral, who got to stay in the Presidential suite?

14. Who was the first President appointed to the Supreme Court?

15. From what educational institute did Ulysses S. Grant receive a degree?

16. Jame Knox Polk planned to give his inaugural address outdoors but it rained. Where did he give his inaugural address?

17. What was the number of the last patrol boat that Lt. John F. Kennedy commanded in the Solomon Islands during World War II?

18. What President didn't live in the White House, but his First Lady did?

19. Who was the only First Lady who was not married?

The Answers

QUIZ 1: RECORDS (Introductory Quiz) ___

1. George Washington; 2. Ronald Reagan or _____; 3. John Adams; 4. Woodrow Wilson; 5. Abraham Lincoln; 6. James Madison; 7. William Howard Taft; 8. John Adams; 9. John F. Kennedy; 10. Grover Cleveland.

QUIZ 2: ACTORS ___

1. Franklin D. Roosevelt; 2. Helen Gahagan (Douglas); 3. Laura Keene; 4. Ty Hardin; 5. John Wilkes Booth; 6. Eleven; 7. John Tyler; 8. Patricia Ryan Nixon; 9. Edwin Booth; 10. Gerald Ford; 11. Robert De Niro (as Travis Bickle) and Jodie Foster; 12. Lyndon B. Johnson; 13. Patti Davis (daughter of Ronald Reagan and Nancy Davis Reagan); 14. Jane Wyman, Ronald Reagan's ex-wife (for *Johnny Belinda*); 15. Richard Boone.

QUIZ 3: ADOPTIONS/STEPPARENTS ___

1. Andrew Jackson; 2. Andrew Jackson and Herbert Hoover; 3. Andrew Jackson; 4. Abraham Lincoln; 5. Millard Fillmore, Warren G. Harding, and Calvin Coolidge; 6. Michael Reagan; 7. James Buchanan; 8. Andrew Jackson and Gerald Ford; 9. Gerald Ford (born Leslie King, Jr.); 10. Eleanor Roosevelt.

QUIZ 4: ADVICE ___

1. Grover Cleveland (D); 2. Calvin Coolidge (A); 3. Franklin D. Roosevelt (C)

QUIZ 5: AGES ___

1. Theodore Roosevelt (at forty-two); 2. John F. Kennedy (at forty-three); 3. Thirty-five; 4. Thirty-five; 5. Harry S Truman (at sixty); 6. John Adams and Herbert Hoover; 7. Forty-eight; 8. Fifty-five; 9. Ronald Reagan; 10. James Madison; 11. Dwight D. Eisenhower; 12. John F. Kennedy (forty-three) and Dwight D. Eisenhower (seventy-one); 13. Grover Cleveland; 14. James Madison; 15. Bess Truman; 16. Benjamin

Harrison; 17. Seventy years old; 18. Nineteen years old; 19. Thomas Jefferson; 20. John F. Kennedy.

QUIZ 6: ALL IN THE FAMILY _____

1. John Adams; 2. Benjamin Harrison; 3. Franklin D. Roosevelt; 4. John Adams and John Quincy Adams; 5. William Henry Harrison and Benjamin Harrison; 6. Elliot Roosevelt (brother of Theodore Roosevelt and father of Eleanor Roosevelt); 7. Abigail Adams (mother of John Quincy Adams); 8. John Scott Harrison; 9. John F. Kennedy and Robert F. Kennedy; 10. David Eisenhower (grandson of Dwight D. Eisenhower, and the son-in-law of Richard M. Nixon).

QUIZ 7: AMBASSADORS AND MINISTERS _____

1. John Adams; 2. Thomas Jefferson; 3. John Quincy Adams; 4. Ulysses S. Grant; 5. Gerald Ford; 6. John Quincy Adams and John F. Kennedy; 7. Martin Van Buren; 8. James Monroe; 9. John Quincy Adams; 10. Five; Extra: James Monroe. Extra: Dwight D. Eisenhower (John S.D. Eisenhower).

QUIZ 8: ANCESTORS _____

1. Calvin Coolidge; 2. James Madison and Zachary Taylor; 3. Richard M. Nixon and Jimmy Carter; 4. John Tyler; 5. Abraham Lincoln; 6. Franklin D. Roosevelt; 7. Pocahontas; 8. Theodore Roosevelt and Franklin D. Roosevelt (fifth cousins); 9. John Adams; 10. Ulysses S. Grant; Extra: Zachary Taylor.

QUIZ 9: ANIMALS _____

1. Andrew Johnson; 2. William Howard Taft; 3. Woodrow Wilson; 4. Dwight D. Eisenhower; 5. George Washington; 6. George Washington; 7. Theodore Roosevelt; 8. A raccoon; 9. A grizzly bear; 10. A snake.

QUIZ 10: APPOINTMENTS _____

1. Franklin D. Roosevelt; 2. Franklin D. Roosevelt; 3. Warren G. Harding; 4. Alexander Hamilton; 5. James Wilson; 6. Henry Wallace (his father was Henry Cantwell Wallace); 7. Jimmy Carter; 8. John Astin; 9. John Mitchell; 10. Andrew Mellon.

QUIZ 11: ASSASSINATIONS AND ATTEMPTS _____

1. Gerald Ford; 2. Andrew Jackson; 3. Abraham Lincoln; 4. Franklin D. Roosevelt; 5. Gerald Ford; 6. Theodore Roosevelt; 7. John Garfield; 8. Abraham Lincoln, John Garfield, and William McKinley; 9. Francis Scott Key; 10. 1939.

QUIZ 12: AUTHORS _____

1. John F. Kennedy; 2. Franklin D. Roosevelt; 3. Abraham Lincoln; 4. Martin Van Buren; 5. Ulysses S. Grant; 6. Franklin Pierce; 7. *The Jungle;* 8. Ulysses S. Grant; 9. William McKinley; 10. Jim Bishop.

QUIZ 13: AUTOBIOGRAPHIES _____

1. Herbert Hoover; 2. Jimmy Carter; 3. Martin Van Buren; 4. John Adams; 5. Jimmy Carter and Rosalynn Carter; 6. Eleanor Roosevelt; 7. Betty Ford; 8. Rosalynn Carter; 9. *Where's the Rest of Me?;* 10. Richard M. Nixon (two-volume autobiography, *RN*).

QUIZ 14: AUTOMOBILES _____

1. William Howard Taft; 2. Theodore Roosevelt; 3. A Studebaker; 4. Franklin D. Roosevelt; 5. Harry S Truman; 6. Dwight D. Eisenhower; 7. Woodrow Wilson; 8. A Lincoln; 9. William Howard Taft (1909); 10. Franklin D. Roosevelt (his son Franklin D. Roosevelt, Jr., owned the Roosevelt Fiat Motors of America). Extra: Lyndon B. Johnson.

QUIZ 15: AVIATION _____

1. George Washington; 2. Lyndon B. Johnson; 3. Dwight D. Eisenhower; 4. Theodore Roosevelt (in 1910 when he was a former President); 5. Caroline (named for John F. Kennedy's daughter); 6. Lyndon B. Johnson; 7. Franklin D. Roosevelt; 8. Dwight D. Eisenhower (in 1957); 9. Air Force One; 10. Navy Marine One.

QUIZ 16: AWARDS _____

1. John F. Kennedy; 2. Woodrow Wilson; 3. Theodore Roosevelt; 4. Gerald Ford; 5. Thomas Jefferson; 6. Theodore Roosevelt (he didn't receive it, however); 7. Dwight D. Eisenhower; 8. John F. Kennedy; 9. Harry S Truman; 10. Charles G. Dawes; 11. George Washington (the Congressional Medal on May 25, 1776); 12. George Washington; 13. Abraham Lincoln; 14. Jacqueline Kennedy; 15. Richard M. Nixon (for the Nixon interviews with David Frost).

QUIZ 17: BATTLES _____

1. Andrew Jackson (the Battle of New Orleans); 2. Franklin Pierce; 3. World War I; 4. Rutherford B. Hayes; 5. Zachary Taylor; 6. Franklin Pierce; 7. Theodore Roosevelt; 8. Fort Stevens; 9. Herbert and Lou Hoover; 10. Ulysses S. Grant.

QUIZ 18: BIOGRAPHIES _____

1. Herbert Hoover; 2. Woodrow Wilson; 3. Abraham Lincoln; 4. William Howard Taft; 5. Gerald Ford; 6. Carl Sandburg; 7. Richard M. Nixon (Julie Nixon Eisenhower); 8. Harry S Truman (Margaret Truman); 9. Theodore Roosevelt; 10. Calvin Coolidge.

QUIZ 19: BIRDS _____

1. Canaries; 2. Dolley Madison; 3. James Buchanan (Harriet Lane); 4. Thomas Jefferson; 5. Poll; 6. Abraham Lincoln; 7. William McKinley; 8. Ronald Reagan and Nancy Davis; 9. Abraham Lincoln; 10. The wild turkey.

QUIZ 20: BIRTHPLACES _____

1. Andrew Jackson (March 15, 1767); 2. Herbert Hoover (August 10, 1874); 3. Eight; 4. Ronald Reagan; 5. Andrew Jackson; 6. Abraham Lincoln (born in Hodgenville, Kentucky, February 12, 1809); 7. Theodore Roosevelt; 8. John Adams and John Quincy Adams (Franklin Street, Quincy, Massachusetts); 9. Dwight D. Eisenhower; 10. Lyndon B. Johnson (Johnson City, Texas); 11. Harry S Truman; 12. James Buchanan; 13. New York; 14. William Henry Harrison and John Tyler; 15. Ulysses S. Grant, Rutherford B. Hayes, and James A. Garfield.

QUIZ 21: BIRTHS _____

1. Calvin Coolidge; 2. John F. Kennedy; 3. Richard M. Nixon; 4. Jimmy Carter; 5. Martin Van Buren; 6. Ohio; 7. October (six); 8. June; 9. Chester A. Arthur; 10. Woodrow Wilson; Extra: Abraham Lincoln.

QUIZ 22: BOATS AND SHIPS _____

1. James Monroe (in 1819); 2. Jimmy Carter; 3. PT-109; 4. Gerald Ford (USS *Monterey*); 5. John F. Kennedy (Robert F. Kennedy served on board the USS *Joseph P. Kennedy, Jr.*); 6. *George Washington;* 7. *Mayflower;* 8. *Lusitania;* 9. *Sequoia;* 10. Theodore Roosevelt.

QUIZ 23: BOOKS _____

1. Theodore Roosevelt; 2. John Quincy Adams; 3. Thomas Jefferson; 4. Herbert Hoover; 5. Benjamin Harrison; 6. Joseph P. Kennedy (father of John F. Kennedy); 7. *Why England Slept;* 8. George Bancroft; 9. Grover Cleveland; 10. Theodore Roosevelt; 11. *Crusade In Europe* by Dwight D. Eisenhower and *Profiles In Courage* by John F. Kennedy; 12. Nancy Davis Reagan; 13. Elliott Roosevelt (son of Franklin and Eleanor Roosevelt); 14. Gerald Ford; 15. Theodore H. White.

QUIZ 24: BOYHOOD _____

1. John Adams; 2. James Garfield; 3. Dwight D. Eisenhower; 4. Franklin D. Roosevelt; 5. John F. Kennedy.

QUIZ 25: BREAKING THE LAW _____

1. Ulysses S. Grant; 2. James Buchanan; 3. Ronald Reagan; 4. Franklin Pierce; 5. Andrew Johnson; 6. Ulysses S. Grant; 7. Andrew Jackson; 8. Lynette "Squeaky" Fromme; 9. Albert Fall; 10. John F. Kennedy.

QUIZ 26: BROKEN PROMISES _____

1. Franklin D. Roosevelt; 2. Richard M. Nixon; 3. Ronald Reagan (PATCO); 4. Woodrow Wilson; 5. John F. Kennedy.

QUIZ 27: BROTHERS _____

1. John F. Kennedy (his brother was Robert F. Kennedy); 2. Lyndon B. Johnson (Sam Houston Johnson); 3. Jimmy Carter (his brother was Billy Carter); 4. Thomas Jefferson; 5. Richard M. Nixon (his brother was Donald Nixon); 6. Jimmy Carter (his brother was Billy Carter); 7. Dwight D. Eisenhower; 8. The Chicago Cubs; 9. James Buchanan (Rev. Edward Buchanan) and Grover Cleveland (Rev. William Cleveland); 10. James Madison (Gen. William Madison) and Zachary Taylor (Gen. Joseph P. Taylor); 11. John F. Kennedy (Robert F. Kennedy and Edward Kennedy); 12. William McKinley; 13. Grover Cleveland; 14. Joseph Kennedy, Jr.

QUIZ 28: BURIALS _____

1. Woodrow Wilson; 2. Thomas Jefferson; 3. Lyndon B. Johnson; 4. Billy Graham; 5. Zachary Taylor (Zachary Taylor National Cemetery, near Louisville, Kentucky); 6. New York (nine); 7. George Clinton; 8. Daniel D. Tompkins; 9. Bitburg; 10. Indianapolis, Indiana; Extra: William Howard Taft. Extra: Andrew Johnson.

QUIZ 29: BUSINESS _____

1. Rutherford B. Hayes; 2. Calvin Coolidge; 3. Donald Nixon; 4. Woodrow Wilson; 5. John F. Kennedy (Joseph P. Kennedy).

QUIZ 30: THE CABINET _____

1. Theodore Roosevelt; 2. Franklin Pierce; 3. Abraham Lincoln (Robert Todd Lincoln); 4. John F. Kennedy and Lyndon B. Johnson; 5. Theodore Roosevelt; 6. Lyndon B. Johnson; 7. Herbert Hoover (Herbert Hoover, Jr.); 8. William Howard Taft; 9. James Monroe (Secretary of State and Secretary of War); 10. Andrew Jackson; 11. Henry "Light Horse Harry" Lee; 12. Woodrow Wilson; 13. John Tyler; 14. Herbert Hoover; 15. John F. Kennedy (Robert Strange McNamara); Extra: Dwight D. Eisenhower.

QUIZ 31: CABINET NICKNAMES _____

1. Warren G. Harding (D); 2. Theodore Roosevelt (E); 3. Herbert Hoover (B); 4. Andrew Jackson (A); 5. Franklin D. Roosevelt (C).

QUIZ 32: CAMPAIGN SLOGANS _____

1. Woodrow Wilson; 2. Warren G. Harding; 3. Herbert Hoover; 4. Barry Goldwater; 5. "Give 'em hell, Harry!"; 6. Lyndon Johnson ("All the way with LBJ"); 7. Calvin Coolidge; 8. Pierce (Franklin Pierce); 9. Lady Bird Johnson; 10. "Whip Inflation Now."

QUIZ 33: CAMPAIGN SONGS _____

1. "Happy Days Are Here Again"; 2. John F. Kennedy; 3. Al Jolson; 4. Irving Berlin.

QUIZ 34: CANDIDATES _____

1. Victoria C. Woodhull; 2. Eugene V. Debs; 3. William T. Sherman; 4. James Knox Polk; 5. Horace Greeley; 6. The Socialist Party; 7. Belva Ann Lockwood; 8. Martin Van Buren; 9. Dan Rice; 10. Frederick Douglass.

QUIZ 35: CHILDREN _____

1. John Tyler; 2. John Quincy Adams; 3. John Quincy Adams (George Washington Adams and John Adams); 4. Abraham Lincoln; 5. Calvin Coolidge; Extra: Grover Cleveland and John F. Kennedy.

QUIZ 36: THE CIVIL WAR _____

1. John Tyler; 2. Zachary Taylor; 3. George McClellan; 4. Grover Cleveland; 5. Ulysses S. Grant; 6. Abraham Lincoln; 7. John Quincy Adams (Charles Francis Adams); 8. William McKinley; 9. Rutherford B. Hayes; 10. Andrew Johnson; 11. John C. Breckinridge; 12. Alexander Stephens; 13. Seven; 14. Ulysses G. Grant; 15. James Buchanan (February 4, 1861).

QUIZ 37: CLOSE FRIENDS AND ADVISORS _____

1. John F. Kennedy (A); 2. Richard M. Nixon (C); 3. Franklin D. Roosevelt (D); 4. Woodrow Wilson (B); 5. Ronald Reagan (E).

QUIZ 38: COINCIDENCES _____

1. General Douglas MacArthur; 2. Harry S Truman (he replaced Henry Wallace, and Truman's wife's name was Elizabeth Wallace); 3. USS *Missouri;* 4. Al Capone; 5. Theodore Roosevelt and Franklin D. Roosevelt; 6. Graduating from West Point; 7. Either seven or eight letters; 8. Republican; 9. Edith Wilson (the Woodrow Wilson Bridge); 10. Ronald Wilson Reagan; 11. Lynette "Squeaky" Fromme; 12. John Adams and Thomas Jefferson; 13. John F. Kennedy; 14. Every President has died in office; 15. Aquarius.

QUIZ 39: COLLEGES _____

1. The University of Virginia; 2. Woodrow Wilson; 3. Nine; 4. The College of William and Mary; 5. Ulysses S. Grant; 6. Dwight D. Eisenhower; 7. Woodrow Wilson; 8. Princeton; 9. James Knox Polk; 10. Rutherford B. Hayes; 11. Harry S Truman; 12. Herbert Hoover; 13. John Adams, John Quincy Adams, Theodore Roosevelt, Franklin D. Roosevelt, and John F. Kennedy; 14. Harvard University; 15. William Henry Harrison.

QUIZ 40: COMMITTEES _____

1. Gerald Ford; 2. Richard M. Nixon; 3. Ronald Reagan; 4. Thomas Jefferson, James Madison, and James Monroe; 5. Alben Barkley (under President Harry S Truman); Extra: Abraham Lincoln.

QUIZ 41: CONGRESS _____

1. James A. Garfield; 2. John Quincy Adams; 3. Woodrow Wilson; 4. John Quincy Adams; 5. John Tyler; Extra: Andrew Johnson. Extra: William Henry Harrison and James Garfield.

QUIZ 42: CUSTOMS _____

1. Thomas Jefferson; 2. Twenty-one; 3. Twenty-one (the same as the incumbent President); 4. Abraham Lincoln; 5. George Washington.

QUIZ 43: DATES AND YEARS _____

1. James Knox Polk and Warren G. Harding; 2. January 20; 3. The first Tuesday after the first Monday in November; 4. March 4 (March 5, if the 4th were a Sunday); 5. 1920; 6. Martin Van Buren, William Henry Harrison, and John Tyler; 7. John Adams and Thomas Jefferson; 8. Benjamin Harrison and William McKinley; 9. Fourteen years; 10. Theodore Roosevelt.

QUIZ 44: DAUGHTERS _____

1. Theodore Roosevelt; 2. James Monroe; 3. Lynda Bird, the daughter of Lyndon Johnson, married Chuck Robb; 4. Abigail Adams (born July 14, 1765); 5. Benjamin Harrison; 6. Patti Davis (daughter of Ronald Reagan); 7. Grover Cleveland; 8. Theodore Roosevelt; 9. Grover Cleveland; 10. Woodrow Wilson.

QUIZ 45: DEATHS _____

1. George Washington; 2. John Adams; 3. William Henry Harrison; 4. John Quincy Adams; 5. John F. Kennedy; 6. Eight (four by assassinations); 7. Four (William King, Thomas Hendricks, Garret Hobart, and James Sherman); 8. Rutherford B. Hayes (he died in the arms of his son Webb Hayes); 9. Letitia Tyler, Caroline Harrison, and Ellen Wilson; 10. Harry S Truman and Lyndon B. Johnson.

QUIZ 46: DEBATES _____

1. Stephen Douglas; 2. Richard M. Nixon and Nikita Khrushchev; 3. Lyndon B. Johnson; 4. William McKinley; 5. Abraham Lincoln and Stephen Douglas.

QUIZ 47: DEBTS _____

1. Mary Todd Lincoln (wife of Abraham Lincoln); 2. Ronald Reagan; 3. Warren G. Harding; 4. Frank Sinatra; 5. Andrew Jackson; 6. George Washington; 7. Millard Fillmore; 8. Ronald Reagan; 9. Harry S Truman (who believed a "Truman Plan" wouldn't pass Congress); 10. Jimmy Carter.

QUIZ 48: DEDICATIONS _____

1. Grover Cleveland; 2. John F. Kennedy International Airport; 3. Chester A. Arthur (February 21, 1885); 4. The Francis Scott Key Memorial; 5. Herbert Hoover; Extra: Franklin D. Roosevelt.

QUIZ 49: DESCENDANTS _____

1. Nelson Eddy; 2. Thomas Jefferson; 3. William Henry Harrison; 4. John Breckenridge; 5. Marilyn Monroe.

QUIZ 50: DOCUMENTS _____

1. George Washington and James Madison; 2. The Monroe Doctrine; 3. John Adams and Thomas Jefferson; 4. The passage condemning slavery; 5. James Madison; Extra: The Gettysburg Address. Extra: John Adams.

QUIZ 51: DOGS _____

1. George Washington; 2. George Bush; 3. Franklin D. Roosevelt's Fala on September 23, 1944, and Richard M. Nixon's Checkers on September 23, 1952; 4. Fala (Franklin D. Roosevelt's pet dog); 5. Caswell Laddie Boy; 6. Eleanor Roosevelt; 7. James Monroe; 8. Lucky; 9. Liberty; 10. Him and Her.

QUIZ 52: ELECTIONS _____

1. George Washington; 2. James Monroe; 3. Thomas Jefferson; 4. Rutherford B. Hayes; 5. Andrew Jackson (over John Quincy Adams); 6. Jimmy Carter; 7. John Quincy Adams; 8. Zachary Taylor; 9. Rutherford B. Hayes; 10. One; 11. Zachary Taylor; 12. Richard M. Nixon and Ronald Reagan; 13. George Washington (1789); 14. Aaron Burr; 15. Lyndon B. Johnson; 16. Grover Cleveland; 17. Ten (New York didn't vote in time, and neither Rhode Island nor North Carolina had ratified the Constitution); 18. Andrew Jackson.

QUIZ 53: ESTATES _____

1. George Washington; 2. Monticello (owned by Thomas Jefferson); 3. Andrew Jackson; 4. Franklin D. Roosevelt; 5. Richard M. Nixon; 6. Theodore Roosevelt; 7. James Buchanan; 8. Martin Van Buren; 9. James Monroe; 10. John Tyler; 11. Mount Vernon (owned by George Washington); 12. George Washington (Mount Vernon); 13. Rutherford B. Hayes; 14. The Hermitage; 15. Rancho del Cielo (Ranch in the Sky).

QUIZ 54: FASHION _____

1. Thomas Jefferson; 2. The Ike jacket (Dwight D. Eisenhower); 3. Richard M. Nixon; 4. Brooks Brothers; 5. James Monroe; 6. Zachary Taylor; 7. Andrew Johnson; 8. Lyndon B. Johnson; 9. James Madison; 10. Lady Bird Johnson (February 29, 1968); Extra: Betty Ford.

QUIZ 55: FATHERS _____

1. Warren G. Harding; 2. Rutherford B. Hayes and Andrew Jackson; 3. Franklin Pierce; 4. Calvin Coolidge; 5. John F. Kennedy; 6. Harry S Truman; 7. John Quincy Adams and William Henry Harrison; 8. Three; 9. William Howard Taft; 10. Ministers; 11. Warren G. Harding; 12. Chester A. Arthur; 13. Warren G. Harding and John F. Kennedy; 14. Bess Truman; 15. Thomas Jefferson; Extra: William Howard Taft. Extra: William Henry Harrison and John Tyler.

QUIZ 56: FEDERAL EMPLOYEES _____

1. Andrew Jackson; 2. Chester A. Arthur; 3. Martin Van Buren; 4. Franklin D. Roosevelt; 5. Ronald Reagan; Extra: Theodore Roosevelt. Extra: Rutherford B. Hayes. Extra: Ulysses S. Grant.

QUIZ 57: FIRST LADIES _____

1. Lou Hoover (wife of Herbert Hoover); 2. Jacqueline Kennedy; 3. Louisa Catherine Adams (wife of John Quincy Adams); 4. Gerald Ford; 5. Lou Hoover (wife of Herbert Hoover); 6. Eleanor Roosevelt (who informed Harry S Truman that he was the new President); 7. Rachel Jackson; 8. Dolley Madison; 9. Letitia Tyler (wife of John Tyler); 10. Betty Ford.

QUIZ 58: FIRST LADIES: NICKNAMES AND TITLES _____

1. Elizabeth Monroe (D); 2. Abigail Adams (A); 3. Eleanor Roosevelt (C); 4. Harry S Truman (A); 5. Frankie (B).

QUIZ 59: FIRST LADIES: PORTRAYALS __

1. Frances Folson Cleveland; 2. Greer Garson; 3. Jaclyn Smith; 4. Una Merkel; 5. Geraldine Fitzgerald; 6. Mrs. Florence Harding; 7. Bess Truman; 8. Eleanor Roosevelt; 9. *The Greek Tycoon;* 10. Jane Alexander.

QUIZ 60: FIRSTS _____

1. Harry S Truman; 2. James Knox Polk; 3. Martin Van Buren (1782); 4. James Garfield; 5. Franklin D. Roosevelt (he hosted George VI and Queen Elizabeth II); 6. Zachary Taylor; 7. Gerald Ford; 8. Woodrow Wilson (he defeated William Howard Taft and Theodore Roosevelt); 9. Lyndon B. Johnson (he enlisted on December 9, 1941); 10. Andrew Jackson; Extra: John Tyler.

QUIZ 61: THE FLAG _____

1. Benjamin Harrison; 2. James Monroe; 3. George Washington; 4. Woodrow Wilson; 5. John Nance Gardner; Extra: Richard M. Nixon. Extra: Dwight D. Eisenhower.

QUIZ 62: FOOD AND DRINK _____

1.Thomas Jefferson; 2. John Adams; 3. Andrew Jackson; 4. Lucy Webb Hayes (wife of Rutherford B. Hayes); 5. Thomas Jefferson (at the time tomatoes were believed to be poisonous); 6. Lyndon B. Johnson; 7. Thomas Jefferson; 8. Thomas Jefferson; 9. Thomas Jefferson; 10. Grover Cleveland.

QUIZ 63: FOOTBALL _____

1. Washington and Jefferson (1908); 2. Ronald Reagan; 3. Dwight D. Eisenhower; 4. Richard M. Nixon; 5. Lyndon B. Johnson; 6. Theodore Roosevelt; 7. Franklin D. Roosevelt; 8. Gerald Ford; 9. John F. Kennedy; 10. Paul Warfield; Extra: George "the Gipper" Gipp.

QUIZ 64: FORMER PRESIDENTS _____

1. Four; 2. John Adams; 3. Martin Van Buren in 1848 (Free Soil Party), Millard Fillmore in 1853 (Whig Party), and Theodore Roosevelt in 1916 (Progressive Party); 4. James Knox Polk; 5. Herbert Hoover; Extra: James Madison.

QUIZ 65: FUNERALS _____

1. Henry "Light Horse Harry" Lee; 2. William Howard Taft; 3. Lyndon
B. Johnson; 4. Warm Springs, Georgia, to Washington, D.C., to New
York City; 5. Sam Rayburn; 6. Abraham Lincoln; 7. William Howard
Taft (and his son Robert A. Taft); 8. Richard M. Nixon (who gave
Dwight D. Eisenhower's eulogy); 9. John F. Kennedy; 10. James Gar-
field.

QUIZ 66: GOVERNORS _____

1. Woodrow Wilson; 2. Ronald Reagan; 3. Thomas Jefferson; 4. Andrew
Jackson (neither was injured); 5. William Henry Harrison and John Tyler;
6. Virginia; 7. New York; 8. James Knox Polk; 9. Andrew Johnson; 10.
Rutherford B. Hayes; 11. Jimmy Carter; 12. William Howard Taft; 13.
California; 14. Martin Van Buren; 15. Indiana; 16. Ohio; 17. Andrew
Jackson; 18. William Henry Harrison; 19. Andrew Jackson and Andrew
Johnson; 20. George Clinton.

QUIZ 67: GRANDFATHERS—
GRANDSONS _____

1. Adlai Stevenson (grandson of Adlai Stevenson); 2. Thomas Jefferson;
3. John Tyler; 4. William Henry Harrison and Benjamin Harrison; 5.
Dwight D. Eisenhower (he named Camp David after his grandson David
Eisenhower); 6. Aaron Burr; 7. William McKinley; 8. Michael Reagan
(his daughter is Cameron Reagan); 9. Thomas Jefferson's; 10. John
Tyler; 11. James Madison and Zachary Taylor; 12. Zachary Taylor; 13.
The Navy; 14. Richard M. Nixon; 15. John F. Kennedy; Extra: Abraham
Lincoln.

QUIZ 68: HABITS AND TRAITS _____

1. Calvin Coolidge; 2. Woodrow Wilson; 3. Ulysses S. Grant; 4. Chester
A. Arthur; 5. Ronald Reagan.

QUIZ 69: HANDICAPS ⸻

1. Theodore Roosevelt; 2. Ronald Reagan; 3. John F. Kennedy; 4. John Quincy Adams; 5. She was cross-eyed; Extra: Andrew Jackson. Extra: Ronald Reagan.

QUIZ 70: HEALTH ⸻

1. Grover Cleveland; 2. William McKinley; 3. Woodrow Wilson; 4. Warren G. Harding; 5. Constipation; 6. Theodore Roosevelt; 7. Franklin D. Roosevelt; 8. Smallpox; 9. Andrew Jackson; 10. Andrew Jackson; Extra: Harry S and Bess Truman.

QUIZ 71: HEIGHTS ⸻

1. John Adams (at 5'7"); 2. James Madison; 3. Abraham Lincoln; 4. Franklin at 6'2" (Theodore was 5'10"); 5. Jimmy Carter; 6. James Madison; 7. President Harry S Truman; 8. 6'2"; 9. Neither, since they were the same person—Grover Cleveland, who was 5'11", 10. Richard M. Nixon.

QUIZ 72: HEROISM ⸻

1. Ronald Reagan; 2. Herbert Hoover; 3. John F. Kennedy; 4. George Washington; 5. Lt. Quentin Roosevelt (son of Theodore Roosevelt); 6. Harry S Truman; 7. Lyndon B. Johnson; 8. John F. Kennedy; 9. Ronald Reagan; 10. Ronald Reagan.

QUIZ 73: HISTORY ⸻

1. Richard M. Nixon; 2. Thomas Jefferson; 3. Woodrow Wilson; 4. John Adams (cousin of Samuel Adams); 5. Thomas Jefferson.

QUIZ 74: HOBBIES ⸻

1. George Washington; 2. James Knox Polk; 3. Andrew Johnson; 4. Ulysses S. Grant; 5. Theodore Roosevelt; 6. John Quincy Adams; 7. A billiard table; 8. Martin Van Buren; 9. Warren G. Harding; 10. Agriculture (farming).

QUIZ 75: HOLIDAYS _____

1. New Year's Day; 2. Calvin Coolidge; 3. Levi Morton; 4. John Adams and Thomas Jefferson; 5. Two, George Washington and Abraham Lincoln; 6. John Tyler and Theodore Roosevelt; 7. The Fourth of July; 8. Franklin D. Roosevelt; 9. George Washington's inauguration; 10. Ulysses S. Grant; Extra: Hannibal Hamlin. Extra: Ulysses S. Grant.

QUIZ 76: HOLLYWOOD _____

1. Franklin D. Roosevelt; 2. Ann Harding; 3. John Tyler (Hollywood Cemetery in Richmond, Virginia); 4. Lee Bowan; 5. Marilyn Monroe; 6. Audrey Hepburn; 7. Franklin D. Roosevelt (James Roosevelt); 8. The Screen Actors Guild; 9. Robert Montgomery; 10. Abraham Lincoln.

QUIZ 77: HOMES _____

1. Warren G. Harding; 2. George Washington; 3. James Madison; 4. Blair House; 5. Andrew Jackson, Zachary Taylor, Millard Fillmore, Franklin Pierce, James Buchanan, Abraham Lincoln, and James Garfield; 6. Zachary Taylor; 7. New York City and Philadelphia; 8. Woodrow Wilson; 9. James Knox Polk; 10. Franklin D. Roosevelt.

QUIZ 78: HONORS _____

1. Ronald Reagan; 2. James Knox Polk; 3. Abraham Lincoln; 4. Jackson; 5. Andrew Jackson; 6. George Washington; 7. Gerald Ford; 8. Herbert Hoover (Hooveria); 9. Hoover Dam (after Herbert Hoover); 10. John F. Kennedy; 11. Calvin Coolidge (the 1926 Sesquicentennial half dollar); 12. Herbert Hoover; 13. Lyndon B. Johnson; 14. Thomas Jefferson; 15. Theodore Roosevelt (the teddy bear).

QUIZ 79: HORSES _____

1. Nelson; 2. Ulysses S. Grant; 3. John Tyler; 4. George Washington; 5. Andrew Jackson; 6. Algonquin; 7. Ronald Reagan; 8. Macaroni; 9. Zachary Taylor; 10. John F. Kennedy and Lyndon B. Johnson.

QUIZ 80: HOUSE OF REPRESENTATIVES

1. James Knox Polk, Millard Fillmore, Franklin Pierce, and John Quincy Adams; 2. John F. Kennedy, Lyndon B. Johnson, and Richard M. Nixon; 3. Lyndon B. Johnson; 4. James Knox Polk; 5. James Madison; Extra: Andrew Jackson.

QUIZ 81: INAUGURAL ADDRESSES _____

1. William Henry Harrison; 2. James Knox Polk; 3. Four; 4. John F. Kennedy; 5. Franklin D. Roosevelt; 6. Franklin Pierce; 7. Jimmy Carter; 8. Andrew Johnson; 9. William Henry Harrison; 10. Dwight D. Eisenhower (2,446 and 2,449 words).

QUIZ 82: INAUGURAL BALLS _____

1. Ronald Reagan; 2. Martin Van Buren; 3. James Madison; 4. Franklin D. Roosevelt; 5. Rosalynn Carter; Extra: Richard M. Nixon. Extra: Rutherford B. Hayes. Extra: Rachel Jackson.

QUIZ 83: INAUGURAL PARADES _____

1. Martin Van Buren; 2. Warren G. Harding; 3. Lyndon B. Johnson (he brought along his beagle Him); 4. James Madison; 5. Grover Cleveland; 6. Theodore Roosevelt; 7. James Monroe; 8. Dwight D. Eisenhower; 9. Helen Taft (wife of William Howard Taft); 10. Dolley Madison.

QUIZ 84: INAUGURATIONS _____

1. Thomas Jefferson; 2. Franklin D. Roosevelt; 3. Ronald Reagan; 4. Rutherford B. Hayes, James A. Garfield, Chester A. Arthur, and Benjamin Harrison; 5. Franklin D. Roosevelt; 6. Theodore Roosevelt; 7. William Howard Taft; 8. James Monroe; 9. George Washington (New York and Philadelphia); 10. George Washington and John Adams.

QUIZ 85: INITIALS _____

1. Harry S Truman; 2. Woodrow Wilson, Calvin Coolidge, Herbert Hoover, and Ronald Reagan; 3. Gamaliel; 4. Simpson; 5. John C. Breckinridge and John C. Fremont; 6. Franklin D. Roosevelt (FDR), John F. Kennedy (JFK), and Lyndon B. Johnson (LBJ); 7. Alan; 8. James Abram Garfield and Chester Alan Arthur; 9. James Monroe, James Madison and Andrew Johnson, Andrew Jackson; 10. Seventeen; Extra: Lyndon Baines Johnson (President), Lady Bird Johnson (First Lady), Lynda Bird Johnson (daughter), and Luci Baines Johnson (daughter); Extra: Franklin Delano Roosevelt and Dwight David Eisenhower.

QUIZ 86: IN-LAWS _____

1. Abraham Lincoln; 2. John F. Kennedy (brother-in-law of Peter Lawford); 3. John Tyler; 4. Martin Van Buren; 5. Zachary Taylor; 6. Franklin D. Roosevelt; 7. James Monroe; 8. Five; 9. Richard M. Nixon (his daughter Julie, married David Eisenhower II, the grandson of President Dwight Eisenhower); 10. Arnold Schwarzenegger; Extra: Sargent Shriver. Extra: Woodrow Wilson.

QUIZ 87: INVENTIONS _____

1. Thomas Jefferson; 2. Abraham Lincoln; 3. Richard M. Nixon; 4. Alexander Graham Bell; 5. Theodore Roosevelt (and/or) Franklin D. Roosevelt (the man was Nicholas Roosevelt).

QUIZ 88: INVENTIONS OF THOMAS JEFFERSON _____

Swivel chair (A); lazy Susan (C); pedometer (E); folding chair (F); hemp machine (I); and an improved plow (J).

QUIZ 89: LAND ACQUISITIONS _____

1. Thomas Jefferson (1803); 2. James Monroe (1819); 3. James Knox Polk; 4. Andrew Johnson (1867); 5. Mexico; 6. James Knox Polk; 7. Millard Fillmore; 8. Franklin Pierce; 9. William McKinley; 10. Denmark.

QUIZ 90: LANGUAGES _____

1. Martin Van Buren; 2. John F. Kennedy; 3. James A. Garfield; 4. Woodrow Wilson; 5. Herbert Hoover's wife, Lou; 6. Thomas Jefferson; 7. John Adams; 8. Rachel Jackson and Abigail Fillmore; 9. Ellen Wilson; 10. Jacqueline Kennedy (when she married Aristotle Onassis).

QUIZ 91: LASTS _____

1. Millard Fillmore (he was a Whig); 2. Franklin D. Roosevelt; 3. Ronald Reagan; 4. Herbert Hoover; 5. James A. Garfield; Extra: Chester A. Arthur. Extra: Warren G. Harding.

QUIZ 92: LAST WORDS _____

1. John Quincy Adams; 2. Woodrow Wilson; 3. John Tyler; 4. James Knox Polk; 5. Dwight D. Eisenhower; 6. James Madison; 7. John F. Kennedy; 8. George Washington; 9. Ulysses S. Grant; 10. William McKinley; 11. Millard Fillmore; 12. Franklin D. Roosevelt; 13. Theodore Roosevelt; 14. Rutherford B. Hayes; 15. William Henry Harrison.

QUIZ 93: THE LAW _____

1. James Monroe; 2. Gerald Ford (in Lynette Fromme's trial for attempted assassination); 3. Thomas Jefferson; 4. Theodore Roosevelt; 5. Lew Wallace (author of *Ben Hur*); 6. Martin Van Buren; 7. Grover Cleveland; 8. Chester A. Arthur; 9. Andrew Johnson; 10. William McKinley; Extra: John Adams.

QUIZ 94: LEGENDS AND RUMORS _____

1. He chopped down a cherry tree; 2. Chester A. Arthur; 3. Grover Cleveland; 4. Warren G. Harding; 5. Thomas Jefferson; 6. Andrew Jackson; 7. Martin Van Buren; 8. Warren G. Harding; 9. Abraham Lincoln (his mother was Nancy Hanks); 10. H. L. Mencken.

QUIZ 95: LIBRARIES _____

1. Harry S Truman; 2. Herbert Hoover; 3. Millard Fillmore; 4. Millard Fillmore (in 1851); 5. The Gerald R. Ford Library; 6. The B'nai B'rith Klutznick Museum; 7. Thomas Jefferson; 8. Franklin D. Roosevelt; 9. The Thomas Jefferson Building (main building), The John Adams Building, and The James Madison Building; 10. The Library of Congress.

QUIZ 96: LINCOLN–KENNEDY SIMILARITIES _____

1. Friday; 2. Johnson; 3. 1908; 4. 1946; 5. 1913.

QUIZ 97: LOSERS _____

1. Henry Clay; 2. She was the first female Presidential candidate (1872); 3. Estes Kefauver; 4. Richard M. Nixon; 5. Charles Evans Hughes; Extra: Jimmy Carter (his brother Billy lost in 1976).

QUIZ 98: MAGAZINES _____

1. Jimmy Carter; 2. Franklin D. Roosevelt; 3. Ronald Reagan; 4. Gerald Ford; 5. *Life* magazine; 6. Eleanor Roosevelt; 7. Gerald Ford; 8. Theodore Roosevelt; 9. Woodrow Wilson; 10. Lyndon B. Johnson; Extra: Richard M. Nixon.

QUIZ 99: MARRIAGES _____

1. James Buchanan (he never married); 2. Grover Cleveland; 3. John Tyler; 4. James Buchanan; 5. He was promoted to first lieutenant; 6. David Eisenhower (grandson of Dwight D. Eisenhower, he married Julia Nixon, the daughter of Richard M. Nixon); 7. Aaron Burr; 8. Andrew Johnson (he was eighteen); 9. Thomas Jefferson; 10. Woodrow Wilson; 11. Benjamin Harrison; 12. Six; 13. Five; 14. John Tyler, Grover Cleveland, and Woodrow Wilson; 15. William Howard Taft; 16. James Madison and Grover Cleveland; 17. John Quincy Adams and Theodore Roosevelt; 18. Andrew Jackson and Warren G. Harding; 19. Abraham

Lincoln (Magistrate Mordecai Lincoln); 20. Herbert Hoover, Richard M. Nixon, and Ronald Reagan.

QUIZ 100: MAYORS _____

1. Grover Cleveland; 2. Calvin Coolidge; 3. John F. Kennedy; 4. Hubert Humphrey; 5. Theodore Roosevelt; 6. Chicago; 7. Andrew Johnson; 8. William Tryon; 9. Grover Cleveland; 10. William Howard Taft.

QUIZ 101: MEETINGS _____

1. President Franklin D. Roosevelt, Prime Minister Winston Churchill, and Premier Joseph Stalin; 2. President Harry S Truman, Prime Minister Clement Attlee, and Premier Joseph Stalin; 3. Dumbarton Oaks, in Georgetown, Washington, D.C.; 4. Camp David; 5. Venice.

QUIZ 102: MILITARY _____

1. James Madison; 2. Fort Necessity; 3. James Buchanan (private); 4. James Garfield; 5. Dwight D. Eisenhower; 6. Rutherford B. Hayes; 7. John Adams; 8. George Washington; 9. Winfield Scott and Zachary Taylor; 10. George Washington and Ulysses S. Grant; 11. Dwight D. Eisenhower; 12. Ulysses S. Grant, Rutherford B. Hayes, and James A. Garfield; 13. Ulysses S. Grant; 14. Andrew Jackson (as a boy); 15. Dwight D. Eisenhower.

QUIZ 103: MINORITIES _____

1. Booker T. Washington; 2. Lyndon B. Johnson; 3. Eleanor Roosevelt; 4. Dwight D. Eisenhower; 5. Sandra Day O'Connor; 6. Abraham Lincoln; 7. Harry S Truman; 8. Republican Senator Margaret Chase Smith (1964); 9. Lyndon B. Johnson; 10. Jimmy Carter.

QUIZ 104: MISTAKES _____

1. St. Patrick's Day; 2. Gerald Ford; 3. Ronald Reagan; 4. John Adams; 5. The Gettysburg Address.

QUIZ 105: MONEY _____

1. Thomas Jefferson; 2. Martin Van Buren; 3. George Washington; 4. John Tyler; 5. $200,000; 6. $25,000; 7. $50,000; 8. $75,000; 9. $100,000; 10. Richard M. Nixon; Extra: Andrew Carnegie. Extra: James Knox Polk. Extra: Herbert Hoover and John F. Kennedy.

QUIZ 106: MONUMENTS/MEMORIALS __

1. Left to right they are George Washington, Thomas Jefferson, Abraham Lincoln, and Theodore Roosevelt; 2. David Rice Atchison; 3. Abraham Lincoln; 4. Theodore Roosevelt; 5. Franklin D. Roosevelt; 6. Theodore Roosevelt (Theodore Roosevelt Island); 7. Ulysses S. Grant; 8. Eleven; 9. The Lincoln Memorial; 10. William Howard Taft (his son was honored with the Robert A. Taft Memorial).

QUIZ 107: MOTHERS _____

1. Jimmy Carter (his mother is Lillian Carter); 2. Harry S Truman; 3. Abraham Lincoln; 4. Franklin D. Roosevelt; 5. James Knox Polk; 6. James A. Garfield; 7. Franklin D. Roosevelt; 8. Woodrow Wilson (son of Janet Woodrow); 9. James Knox Polk, Thomas Woodrow Wilson, Franklin Delano Roosevelt, John Fitzgerald Kennedy, Lyndon Baines Johnson, Richard Milhous Nixon, and Ronald Wilson Reagan; 10. Ulysses Simpson Grant (born Hiram Ulysses Grant).

QUIZ 108: MOTION PICTURES _____

1. *Hellcats of the Navy;* 2. Franklin D. Roosevelt; 3. Neil; 4. Five; 5. William McKinley (by the Biograph Company in 1896); 6. *Birth of a Nation* (1916); 7. Franklin D. Roosevelt; 8. *Taxi Driver;* 9. *The Story of G. I. Joe;* 10. Richard M. Nixon; Extra: Philip Dunne. Extra: John F. Kennedy.

QUIZ 109: MOTTOES AND SLOGANS __

1. Thomas Jefferson; 2. Theodore Roosevelt; 3. George Washington; 4. Harry S Truman; 5. Ronald Reagan.

QUIZ 110: MUSIC _____

1. Ulysses S. Grant; 2. John F. Kennedy; 3. Harry S Truman; 4. Woodrow Wilson; 5. The violin; 6. Herbert Hoover (1931); 7. John Tyler; 8. A piano; 9. Abraham Lincoln; 10. Warren G. Harding.

QUIZ 111: NAMES _____

1. Hiram; 2. James Madison, James Monroe, James Buchanan, James A. Garfield, James Knox Polk, and James Carter; 3. John Adams, John Quincy Adams, John Tyler, and John F. Kennedy (John Calvin Coolidge is also correct); 4. William Henry Harrison, William McKinley, and William Howard Taft; 5. Stephen; 6. Dwight David Eisenhower, born David Dwight Eisenhower; 7. Ulysses S. Grant; 8. Lyndon B. Johnson (he was called Baby); 9. George Washington (named for King George); 10. Thomas Jefferson and (Thomas) Woodrow Wilson; 11. Teddy; 12. Adams, Harrison, Johnson, and Roosevelt; 13. Andrew Johnson (named after war hero Andrew Jackson); 14. Gerald Ford (born Leslie King, Jr.); 15. James A. Garfield; 16. Grover Cleveland; 17. George Mifflin Dallas; 18. Eleanor; 19. Anna; Extra: John Quincy Adams (his son was George Washington Adams).

QUIZ 112: NATURE _____

1. Theodore Roosevelt; 2. Chester A. Arthur (Arthur Peak); 3. Yellowstone National Park; 4. Gerald Ford; 5. Devil's Tower; Extra: Jimmy Carter. Extra: Zachary Taylor and William McKinley.

QUIZ 113: THE NAVY _____

1. George Washington; 2. Jimmy Carter; 3. Frank Knox; 4. James V. Forrestal; 5. John Adams; 6. Millard Fillmore; 7. John Tyler; 8. Napoleon Bonaparte; 9. Herbert Hoover; 10. John F. Kennedy, Lyndon B. Johnson, Richard M. Nixon, Gerald Ford, and Jimmy Carter.

QUIZ 114: NEXT-IN-LINE _____

1. Vice President (P); 2. Speaker of the House (N); 3. President Pro Tempore of the Senate (G); 4. Secretary of State (C); 5. Secretary of the Treasury (E); 6. Secretary of Defense (J); 7. Attorney General (O); 8. Secretary of the Interior (D); 9. Secretary of Agriculture (A); 10. Secretary of Commerce (F); 11. Secretary of Labor (L); 12. Secretary of Health and Human Services (H); 13. Secretary of Housing and Urban Development (M); 14. Secretary of Transportation (B); 15. Secretary of Energy (K); 16. Secretary of Education (I).

QUIZ 115: NICKNAMES #1 _____

1. John Adams; 2. Thomas Jefferson; 3. James Madison; 4. Ronald Reagan; 5. James "Jimmy" Carter; 6. James Knox Polk; 7. Herbert Hoover (Hoovervilles); 8. John F. Kennedy; 9. John Quincy Adams; 10. The Happy Warrior.

QUIZ 116: NICKNAMES #2 _____

1. Franklin Pierce (I); 2. Martin Van Buren (G); 3. Theodore Roosevelt (B); 4. John Tyler (C); 5. Andrew Jackson (J); 6. Richard M. Nixon (D); 7. John Adams (E); 8. Calvin Coolidge (A); 9. Abraham Lincoln (F); 10. Thomas Jefferson (H).

QUIZ 117: NOMINATIONS _____

1. Franklin Pierce; 2. Chicago; 3. He was, at the age of eighty, the oldest man ever nominated for President; 4. Franklin D. Roosevelt (on July 2, 1932); 5. James A. Garfield; Extra: William Jennings Bryan. Extra: Millard Fillmore. Extra: Charles O'Conor (1872).

QUIZ 118: NUMBERS _____

1. Seventy-seven; 2. Eight (four by assassins); 3. Five (Abraham Lincoln, Ulysses S. Grant, Rutherford B. Hayes, James A. Garfield, and Benjamin Harrison); 4. Nine; 5. Theodore Roosevelt (while on safari in

Africa); 6. Thirty-five; 7. Only those still living; 8. Abraham Lincoln (until then they were not numbered); 9. Martin Van Buren; 10. Martin Van Buren; Extra: John Tyler.

QUIZ 119: OATHS _____

1. Dwight D. Eisenhower; 2. "Swear" and "affirm"; 3. Franklin Pierce; 4. William Rufus King; 5. "So help me God" 6. Calvin Coolidge and Herbert Hoover; 7. Article II; 8. Harry S Truman; 9. On board Air Force One; 10. It doesn't stipulate; 11. George Washington; 12. John Marshall; 13. George Washington and Chester A. Arthur; 14. Thomas Jefferson; 15. John Quincy Adams.

QUIZ 120: OCCUPATIONS #1 _____

1. George Washington (H); 2. Andrew Jackson (J); 3. Herbert Hoover (F); 4. Gerald Ford (G); 5. Harry S Truman (I); 6. Warren G. Harding (B); 7. Ronald Reagan (A); 8. Woodrow Wilson (C); 9. Abraham Lincoln (D); 10. Lyndon B. Johnson (E).

QUIZ 121: OCCUPATIONS #2 _____

1. Andrew Johnson; 2. Lyndon B. Johnson; 3. Herbert Hoover; 4. Abraham Lincoln and Harry S Truman; 5. William Howard Taft; Extra: Ulysses S. Grant, Rutherford B. Hayes, James A. Garfield, Chester A. Arthur, and Benjamin Harrison.

QUIZ 122: ONLY _____

1. Andrew Johnson; 2. George Washington; 3. Ronald Reagan; 4. Richard M. Nixon; 5. Grover Cleveland; 6. Benjamin Harrison; 7. Dwight D. Eisenhower; 8. Thomas Jefferson (he defeated John Adams); 9. Andrew Jackson; 10. James A. Garfield; Extra: Harry S Truman. Extra: Eleanor Roosevelt.

QUIZ 123: OPPONENTS _____

1. Adlai E. Stevenson; 2. Norman Thomas (Socialist Party); 3. William McKinley; 4. William Howard Taft and Charles Evans Hughes; 5. John Nance Garner.

QUIZ 124: ORGANIZATIONS _____

1. Chester A. Arthur; 2. Gerald Ford; 3. Ronald Reagan; 4. Harry S Truman; 5. John F. Kennedy; 6. Herbert Hoover; 7. William Howard Taft; 8. Thirteen; 9. George Washington; 10. Harry S Truman.

QUIZ 125: OTHER PEOPLE _____

1. Abraham Lincoln; 2. Harry S Truman; 3. Gerald Ford; 4. Abraham Lincoln and James A. Garfield; 5. Presidential bodyguard; 6. He was the only man to have been the son of one President and the father of another; 7. Thomas Hart Benton (he and his brother shot Andrew Jackson, and he was the father-in-law of John C. Fremont); 8. Warren G. Harding; 9. To Henry Kissinger; 10. Abraham Lincoln.

QUIZ 126: OTHER PRESIDENTS _____

1. Fourteen; 2. Peyton Randolph; 3. John Hanson (1781–1782); 4. John Jay; 5. John Hancock; 6. David Rice Atchison (President Pro Tempore of the Senate); 7. Thomas W. Terry; 8. Senator Ben Wade of Ohio; 9. Sam Houston; 10. Jefferson Davis.

QUIZ 127: OVAL OFFICE _____

1. Queen Victoria; 2. The Buck Stops Here; 3. Herbert Hoover; 4. John F. Kennedy; 5. Rutherford B. Hayes.

QUIZ 128: PAINTINGS/PORTRAITS _____

1. Lyndon B. Johnson; 2. Martin Luther King, Jr.; 3. John Quincy Adams; 4. Dolley Madison; 5. Dwight D. Eisenhower; 6. Norman Rock-

well; 7. Elizabeth Shoumantoff; 8. James Buchanan; 9. Gilbert Stuart; 10. In the White House; Extra: Jacqueline Kennedy.

QUIZ 129: PARDONS ⸻⸻⸻⸻⸻

1. Warren G. Harding; 2. Jimmy Carter; 3. Jimmy Carter; 4. Gerald Ford pardoned Richard Nixon; 5. Samuel Mudd; 6. Patty Hearst; 7. George Washington; 8. Impeachment; 9. Theodore Roosevelt; 10. Iva Toguri D'Aquino (Tokyo Rose).

QUIZ 130: PERSONAL APPEARANCE ⸻

1. William Howard Taft; 2. Abraham Lincoln; 3. James Madison; 4. William Howard Taft; 5. George Washington; 6. George Washington; 7. William McKinley; 8. Jimmy Carter; 9. Ronald Reagan; 10. Andrew Jackson.

QUIZ 131: PHOTOGRAPHS ⸻⸻⸻⸻

1. John Quincy Adams; 2. Abraham Lincoln; 3. Calvin Coolidge; 4. Herbert Hoover; 5. Elliot Roosevelt; 6. Abraham Zapruder; 7. Jacqueline Kennedy; 8. Gerald Ford; 9. Lauren Bacall; 10. James Knox Polk (by Mathew Brady in 1849).

QUIZ 132: PLACES ⸻⸻⸻⸻⸻⸻

1. Monrovia, named after James Monroe; 2. Washington; 3. Theodore Roosevelt (Rio Roosevelt); 4. Paris, France; 5. Campobello, Canada; Extra: South Dakota.

QUIZ 133: POLITICAL OFFICES ⸻⸻⸻

1. Andrew Johnson; 2. Woodrow Wilson; 3. Harry S Truman; 4. John Quincy Adams; 5. Richard M. Nixon; Extra: Assistant Secretary of the Navy.

QUIZ 134: POLITICAL PARTIES _____

1. The Federalist Party; 2. Ronald Reagan; 3. The Democratic-Republican Party; 4. The Progressive Party; 5. President John Adams and Vice President Thomas Jefferson; 6. The Bull Moose Party (Progessive Party); 7. The Know-Nothing Party; 8. The Whigs; 9. John C. Fremont; 10. Richard M. Nixon; 11. Abraham Lincoln; 12. Andrew Jackson; 13. The Federalist Party; 14. The Anti-Masonic Party (Baltimore, Maryland); 15. The Democratic Party.

QUIZ 135: POLITICAL SLOGANS _____

1. Franklin Pierce; 2. Barry Goldwater; 3. William McKinley; 4. James Knox Polk; 5. Herbert Hoover; Extra: William Henry Harrison and John Tyler.

QUIZ 136: PORTRAITS ON COINS _____

1. Half Dollar (E); 2. Dime (C); 3. Penny (A); 4. Quarter (D); 5. Nickle (B); 6. Dollar (F); Extra: George Washington, Thomas Jefferson, and Abraham Lincoln.

QUIZ 137: PORTRAITS ON CURRENCY _

1. $1 bill (E); 2. $2 bill (A); 3. $5 bill (I); 4. $20 bill (B); 5. $50 bill (H); 6. $500 bill (C); 7. $1000 bill (G); 8. $5000 bill (D); 9. $100,000 bill (F); Extra: Martha Washington (the 1891 one dollar silver certificate).

QUIZ 138: PORTRAITS ON SAVINGS BONDS _____

1. $10,000 (H); 2. $1000 (G); 3. $500 (F); 4. $25 (A); 5. $75 (C); 6. $100 (D); 7. $200 (E); 8. $50 (B).

QUIZ 139: POSTAGE STAMPS _____

1. James Knox Polk; 2. George Washington (issued in 1847); 3. Franklin Pierce and Franklin D. Roosevelt; 4. Abraham Lincoln; 5. Zachary Taylor; 6. Warren G. Harding; 7. John F. Kennedy; 8. John F. Kennedy (his son John was depicted on a stamp as a little boy waving a flag at the funeral of his father; the other living person was one of the survivors among the soldiers who raised the flag at Iwo Jima during World War II); 9. 1938; 10. Calvin Coolidge.

QUIZ 140: PRESIDENTIAL PORTRAYALS

1. Franklin D. Roosevelt (in the 1942 film *Yankee Doodle Dandy*); 2. Ralph Bellamy; 3. Sidney Blackmer; 4. Theodore Roosevelt (he portrayed Theodore Roosevelt, Jr.); 5. Jimmy Carter; Extra: Gerald Ford.

QUIZ 141: PRESIDENTIAL RELATIONSHIPS _____

1. Zachary Taylor; 2. Martin Van Buren; 3. William Howard Taft and Herbert Hoover; 4. Ulysses S. Grant; 5. Grover Cleveland; Extra: James Madison. Extra: Harry S Truman. Extra: Franklin D. Roosevelt.

QUIZ 142: PRESIDENTS OF FICTION—MOVIES _____

1. Franchot Tone; 2. Peter Sellers; 3. Craig Jones; 4. *The Greek Tycoon;* 5. Bob Newhart; 6. Henry Fonda; 7. Jason Robards, Jr.; 8. *Superman;* 9. Tex Ritter (his son is actor John Ritter); 10. Donald Pleasance.

QUIZ 143: THE PRESS _____

1. Woodrow Wilson (1913); 2. Martin Van Buren; 3. Warren G. Harding; 4. John F. Kennedy; 5. *My Day;* 6. Franklin D. Roosevelt; 7. William Howard Taft; 8. John F. Kennedy; 9. *Chicago Daily Tribune;* 10. Jacqueline Kennedy; 11. Tricky Dick; 12. Calvin Coolidge ("Think-

ing Things Over With Calvin Coolidge"); 13. Horace Greeley; 14. Drew Pearson; 15. Bob Woodward and Carl Bernstein.

QUIZ 144: PROGRAMS _____

1. New Frontier (D); 2. The New Deal (B); 3. The Square Deal (G); 4. New Foundation (E); 5. New Freedom (H); 6. The Great Society (A); 7. Fair Deal (K); 8. Back to Normalcy (F); 9. Peace and Prosperity (I); 10. Era of Good Feeling (J); 11. A New Beginning (C).

QUIZ 145: PROTECTION _____

1. Eleanor Roosevelt; 2. John Parker; 3. Allan Pinkerton; 4. William McKinley; 5. 1951; Extra: Mamie Eisenhower. Extra: 180 agents.

QUIZ 146: QUOTATIONS ABOUT PRESIDENTS _____

1. Henry Knox; 2. Henry Lee; 3. Abraham Lincoln; 4. Theodore Roosevelt; 5. Robert F. Kennedy (about Lyndon B. Johnson).

QUIZ 147: QUOTATIONS ABOUT THE WHITE HOUSE _____

1. First Lady Rachel Donelson (E); 2. Calvin Coolidge (C); 3. Theodore Roosevelt (D); 4. Harry S Truman (A); 5. William Howard Taft (B).

QUIZ 148: QUOTATIONS BY PRESIDENTS _____

1. John F. Kennedy; 2. Theodore Roosevelt; 3. Calvin Coolidge; 4. Ronald Reagan; 5. Andrew Jackson; 6. Abraham Lincoln; 7. Martin Van Buren; 8. Dwight D. Eisenhower: 9. Lyndon B. Johnson; 10. Theodore Roosevelt.

QUIZ 149: QUOTATIONS FROM ONE PRESIDENT ABOUT ANOTHER PRESIDENT _____

1. Richard M. Nixon; 2. Thomas Jefferson; 3. Thomas Jefferson; 4. Abraham Lincoln; 5. John Adams.

QUIZ 150: RADIO _____

1. Warren G. Harding (at the Minnesota State Fair in 1920); 2. World of Chiropractic; 3. Franklin D. Roosevelt (in 1934); 4. Franklin D. Roosevelt; 5. Warren G. Harding (in 1921); 6. Dwight D. Eisenhower; 7. WHO; 8. Ronald Reagan (August 11, 1984); 9. *Love Is on the Air;* 10. *Hollywood Hotel*.

QUIZ 151: RAILROADS _____

1. Andrew Jackson (in 1833); 2. Franklin Pierce; 3. William Howard Taft; 4. Franklin D. Roosevelt (in 1937); 5. James A. Garfield; 6. Edwin Booth (brother of John Wilkes Booth); 7. Harry S Truman; 8. Harry S Truman; 9. Franklin D. Roosevelt; 10. *The Peanut Special;* 11. Abraham Lincoln; 12. William Henry Harrison (in 1841); 13. Rutherford B. Hayes; 14. Abraham Lincoln (Robert Todd Lincoln); 15. Andrew Jackson (in 1837).

QUIZ 152: RE-ELECTIONS _____

1. William Henry Harrison, Rutherford B. Hayes, Benjamin Harrison, Warren G. Harding, and Herbert Hoover; 2. The Twenty-second Amendment; 3. Martin Van Buren; 4. Secretary of State; 5. Ulysses S. Grant and Theodore Roosevelt; 6. James Knox Polk; 7. John Adams; 8. Seven; 9. James Buchanan; 10. Franklin Pierce; Extra: James Monroe.

QUIZ 153: RELATIVES _____

1. George Washington; 2. Thomas Jefferson; 3. John Adams (he defeated Samuel Adams in 1779); 4. John Adams and John Quincy Adams; 5. William Holden; 6. James A. Garfield; 7. Richard M. Nixon; 8. Franklin D. Roosevelt; 9. His niece; 10. William Howard Taft.

QUIZ 154: RELIGION _____

1. Thomas Jefferson; 2. James Knox Polk; 3. James A. Garfield; 4. Herbert Hoover and Richard M. Nixon; 5. Episcopalian; 6. Presbyterian; 7. Seven; 8. John F. Kennedy; 9. John Quincy Adams.

QUIZ 155: RETREATS _____

1. Warm Springs, Georgia; 2. Shangri-La (After James Hilton's novel *Lost Horizon*); 3. Camp David (after his grandson); 4. Anderson Cottage (the "Summer White House"); 5. San Clemente Island off the coast of California.

QUIZ 156: ROMANCES _____

1. John F. Kennedy (Joseph P. Kennedy); 2. George Washington; 3. Thomas Jefferson; 4. Abraham Lincoln; 5. Kay Summersby; 6. Lucy Mercer; 7. Warren G. Harding; 8. John F. Kennedy; 9. Ronald Reagan; 10. Gerald Ford.

QUIZ 157: RUNNING MATES _____

1. Frederick Douglass; 2. Geraldine Ferraro; 3. Curtis Le May; 4. Thomas Eagleton; 5. John Sparkman (1952) and Estes Kefauver (1956).

QUIZ 158: SCANDALS _____

1. Warren G. Harding's administration; 2. Franklin Pierce; 3. James Buchanan; 4. Thomas Jefferson; 5. Grover Cleveland; 6. James Knox Polk; 7. Lyndon B. Johnson ("Landslide Lyndon"); 8. Richard M. Nixon; 9. Richard M. Johnson; 10. Ulysses S. Grant; Extra: Ronald Reagan.

QUIZ 159: SCHOOLING _____

1. Andrew Johnson; 2. Lyndon B. Johnson (Johnson High School); 3. Dwight D. Eisenhower; 4. Harry S Truman; 5. Franklin D. Roosevelt; 6. Franklin D. Roosevelt; 7. The London School of Economics; 8. Andrew Jackson; 9. Calvin Coolidge; 10. Grover Cleveland.

THE PRESIDENTIAL QUIZ BOOK

QUIZ 160: SECONDS ─────────

1. Franklin D. Roosevelt; 2. James A. Garfield; 3. John Tyler (he took over for President William Henry Harrison who died after just thirty-two days in office); 4. Herbert Hoover; 5. John F. Kennedy; Extra: John Adams. Extra: Spiro T. Agnew.

QUIZ 161: SECRETARY OF STATE ─────

1. James Madison; 2, James Monroe; 3. John Quincy Adams; 4. Herbert Hoover; 5. Harry S Truman; 6. Andrew Johnson; 7. Elihu Root; 8. Martin Van Buren; 9. Six; 10. James Monroe; 11. Dwight D. Eisenhower; 12. Cordell Hull (he served from 1933 to 1944); 13. Abel P. Upshur; 14. George C. Marshall; 15. Dean Acheson.

QUIZ 162: SECRETARY OF WAR ─────

1. William Howard Taft; 2. Edwin M. Stanton; 3. Abraham Lincoln (Robert T. Lincoln); 4. Jefferson Davis; 5. John C. Breckinridge; Extra: John B. Floyd. Extra: Tennis's Davis Cup.

QUIZ 163: SECRET SERVICE CODE NAMES ─────────

1. Sandstorm (C)/Nelson Rockefeller; 2. Pinafore (J)/Betty Ford; 3. Volunteer (E)/Lyndon Johnson; 4. Rawhide (B)/Ronald Reagan; 5. Fernlake (I)/Bess Truman; 6. Lancer (A)/John F. Kennedy; 7. Victoria (H)/ Lady Bird Johnson; 8. Pass Key (D)/Gerald Ford; 9. Lace (G)/Jacqueline Kennedy; 10. Rainbow (F)/Nancy Reagan.

QUIZ 164: THE SENATE ─────────

1. Franklin Pierce; 2. Andrew Johnson; 3. Thomas Hart Benton shot and wounded Andrew Jackson; 4. John F. Kennedy (he defeated Henry Cabot Lodge II, whose grandfather, Henry Cabot Lodge, defeated John F. Fitzgerald, the grandfather of John F. Kennedy); 5. Lyndon B. Johnson; 6. Warren G. Harding; 7. Richard M. Johnson; 8. James Monroe; 9.

Dolley Madison; 10. Six; 11. John C. Calhoun; 12. Ten; 13. Warren G. Harding and John F. Kennedy; 14. James A. Garfield; 15. 101 votes (If fifty senators vote for and fifty senators vote against, the Vice President casts the 101st and tie-breaking vote).

QUIZ 165: SISTERS

1. Thomas Jefferson; 2. Jimmy Carter (written by Ruth Carter Stapleton); 3. John F. Kennedy (his sister Rosemary); 4. Theodore Roosevelt; 5. Thomas Jefferson.

QUIZ 166: SLAVERY

1. Congress deleted it to placate the South; 2. The Emancipation Proclamation; 3. Nine (George Washington, Thomas Jefferson, James Madison, James Monroe, Andrew Jackson, John Tyler, James Knox Polk, Zachary Taylor, and Andrew Jackson); 4. Millard Fillmore; 5. James Monroe (Monrovia); 6. Brazil, Cuba, and the United States; 7. Thomas Jefferson; 8. George Washington; 9. James Monroe; 10. Jefferson Davis; Extra: Chester A. Arthur.

QUIZ 167: SONS

1. John Quincy Adams (George Washington Adams); 2. Theodore Roosevelt; 3. Franklin Pierce; 4. Ronald Reagan (Ron Reagan, Jr.); 5. John; 6. John Tyler; 7. Tad Lincoln; 8. Ulysses S. Grant (Frederick Grant); 9. Theodore Roosevelt; 10. Webb Hayes and Theodore Roosevelt, Jr.; 11. Zachary Taylor; 12. Ronald Reagan (Michael Reagan); 13. Frederick Grant (Ulysses S. Grant) and John Eisenhower (Dwight D. Eisenhower); 14 William Henry Harrison (John Scott Harrison); 15. Martin Van Buren (John Van Buren).

QUIZ 168: SPEECHES

1. James A. Garfield; 2. Franklin D. Roosevelt; 3. Herbert Hoover; 4. Ronald Reagan; 5. James Knox Polk; 6. Theodore Roosevelt; 7. Franklin Pierce; 8. George Washington's Farewell Address; 9. Woodrow Wilson;

10. Freedom of worship, freedom of speech, freedom from want, and freedom from fear; Extra: Harry S Truman. Extra: Theodore Roosevelt.

QUIZ 169: SPORTS ————————————

1. Franklin D. Roosevelt (May 14, 1935); 2. William Howard Taft; 3. George Gipp in the 1940 movie *Knute Rockne—All American* and Grover Cleveland Alexander in the 1952 movie *The Winning Team;* 4. Dwight D. Eisenhower and Gerald Ford; 5. William Howard Taft; 6. Theodore Roosevelt; 7. Bess Truman; 8. Abraham Lincoln; 9. William Howard Taft; 10. Woodrow Wilson; 11. Harry S Truman; 12. Baltimore, Maryland; 13. Dwight D. Eisenhower (for West Point); 14. Franklin D. Roosevelt; 15. Woodrow Wilson in 1915 (Boston Red Sox vs. Philadelphia Phillies).

QUIZ 170: STATES ————————————

1. Jackson (Mississippi), Jefferson City (Missouri), Lincoln (Nebraska), and Madison (Wisconsin); 2. New York; 3. Dwight D. Eisenhower; 4. Richard M. Nixon; 5. Virginia; 6. Colorado; 7. Dwight D. Eisenhower and Lyndon B. Johnson; 8. Lincoln; 9. Vermont, Kentucky, and Tennessee; 10. New Hampshire; Extra: Jackson, Mississippi (named after Andrew Jackson). Extra: Benjamin Harrison's administration (North Dakota, South Dakota, Montana, Washington, Idaho, and Wyoming were admitted); Extra: Lyndon B. Johnson.

QUIZ 171: STATUES ————————————

1. George Washington; 2. George Washington; 3. Thomas Jefferson; 4. Andrew Jackson (in Lafayette Square, Washington, D.C., January 8, 1853); 5. George Washington, Jefferson Davis, Andrew Jackson, and James Garfield; Extra: George Washington. Extra: Laddie Boy (pet dog of President Warren G. Harding).

QUIZ 172: STRIKES ————————————

1. Ronald Reagan; 2. Ronald Reagan; 3. Ronald Reagan; 4. Rutherford B. Hayes; 5. Grover Cleveland; Extra: Calvin Coolidge.

QUIZ 173: SUPREME COURT _____

1. William Howard Taft; 2. John Adams (1797); 3. Andrew Jackson; 4. Sandra Day O'Connor; 5. Abraham Lincoln; 6. John Marshall; 7. Byron White; 8. Earl Warren; 9. George Washington; 10. Hugo L. Black; 11. Richard M. Nixon; 12. Andrew Johnson; 13. John Adams; 14. Richard M. Nixon (1969); 15. Franklin D. Roosevelt.

QUIZ 174: TEACHERS _____

1. Millard Fillmore; 2. James A. Garfield; 3. Woodrow Wilson; 4. Lyndon B. Johnson; 5. Chester A. Arthur; 6. Jimmy Carter; 7. Grover Cleveland; 8. John Adams; 9. William Howard Taft; 10. Benjamin Harrison.

QUIZ 175: TELEPHONE _____

1. William McKinley; 2. Harry S Truman; 3. Grover Cleveland; 4. Rutherford B. Hayes (1878); 5. Lyndon B. Johnson (1967).

QUIZ 176: TELEVISION _____

1. Franklin D. Roosevelt (1939); 2. Dwight D. Eisenhower (1955); 3. Gerald Ford; 4. Richard M. Nixon and John F. Kennedy; 5. Harry S Truman (1947); 6. Dwight D. Eisenhower (1955); 7. John F. Kennedy (1961); 8. Jimmy Carter; 9. Richard M. Nixon; 10. Jimmy Carter; 11. Gerald Ford; 12. Lyndon B. Johnson; 13. Richard M. Nixon; 14. Chicago in 1952 (both the Republican and Democratic Conventions were held there that year); 15. Nancy Reagan; 16. "The Mary Tyler Moore Show"; 17. Everett Dirksen and Gerald Ford; 18. Richard M. Nixon; 19. Mamie Eisenhower; 20. Jacqueline Kennedy.

QUIZ 177: TERMS OF OFFICE _____

1. James Monroe; 2. William Henry Harrison; 3. It limited Presidents to two full terms; 4. Richard M. Nixon; 5. Franklin D. Roosevelt (his first term of office was shortened because the Twentieth Amendment changed

the inauguration date. Roosevelt took over on March 4, 1932, and ended his term on January 20, 1936, less than four years later).

QUIZ 178: TRADITIONS ⎯⎯⎯⎯⎯⎯

1. Chester A. Arthur; 2. Rutherford B. Hayes and his wife, Lucy; 3. William Howard Taft; 4. Dwight D. Eisenhower (1957); 5. She put up the first Christmas tree in the White House; Extra: Caroline Harrison. Extra: Thomas Jefferson.

QUIZ 179: TRAVEL ⎯⎯⎯⎯⎯⎯

1. Theodore Roosevelt (1905); 2. William Howard Taft (1909); 3. Theodore Roosevelt (1906); 4. Woodrow Wilson (1918); 5. Franklin D. Roosevelt; 6. Richard M. Nixon (1972); 7. Dwight D. Eisenhower; 8. Rutherford B. Hayes; 9. John Quincy Adams; 10. Barbados (B).

QUIZ 180: TREATIES ⎯⎯⎯⎯⎯⎯

1. John Adams; 2. John Quincy Adams; 3. The Senate; 4. Jimmy Carter; 5. James Buchanan.

QUIZ 181: TRIOS ⎯⎯⎯⎯⎯⎯

1. James A. Garfield, Harry S Truman, and Gerald Ford; 2. George Washington, Thomas Jefferson, and Martin Van Buren; 3. Martin Van Buren, William Henry Harrison, and John Tyler; 4. John Adams, Thomas Jefferson, and James Monroe; 5. John Adams, John Quincy Adams, and John F. Kennedy; 6. Thomas Jefferson, John Adams, and Martin Van Buren; 7. John Nance Garner, Henry Wallace, and Harry S Truman; 8. Ulysses S. Grant, Rutherford B. Hayes, and James A. Garfield; 9. Rutherford B. Hayes, James A. Garfield, and Chester A. Arthur; 10. Martin Van Buren, Theodore Roosevelt, and Franklin D. Roosevelt.

QUIZ 182: TRUE OR FALSE ⎯⎯⎯⎯⎯⎯

1. True, and he also had teeth made of deer antlers and of whalebone; 2. False, no one can, it's too far across; 3. False; 4. True; 5. False, at age

forty-three John F. Kennedy was the youngest elected President (Theodore Roosevelt was the youngest man, at age forty-two, to *become* President); 6. True (Frank Jr.'s real first name was Franklin, but his father's was Francis); 7. False (he appeared in the 1951 movie *Bedtime for Bonzo,* but not in this sequel); 8. True, seven wives were not married to their husbands when they became President (Martha Jefferson, Rachel Jackson, Hannah Van Buren, Caroline Fillmore, Ellen Arthur, Mary Harrison, and Alice Roosevelt); 9. True; 10. True (he wrote the letter in 1862); Extra: False, the house is based on designs of his birthhouse, which was destroyed by fire in 1779.

QUIZ 183: VETOES _____

1. John C. Calhoun; 2. Twelve; 3. John Tyler; 4. Theodore Roosevelt; 5. Franklin D. Roosevelt; 6. Reapportionment of the House of Representatives according to the 1790 census; 7. Andrew Johnson; 8. Ten days; 9. Andrew Johnson; 10. James Madison; 11. Andrew Johnson (1867); 12. Grover Cleveland; 13. John Tyler (1845); 14. John Adams; 15. Grover Cleveland (584).

QUIZ 184: VICE PRESIDENTS _____

1. Thomas Jefferson; 2. John C. Calhoun; 3. John Tyler; 4. Gerald Ford; 5. Aaron Burr; 6. Harry S Truman; 7. Theodore Roosevelt; 8. William Rufus King (in Cuba); 9. Richard M. Nixon; 10. Martin Van Buren; 11. Hubert Humphrey; 12. William Rufus King; 13. George Clinton (served under Thomas Jefferson and James Madison) and John C. Calhoun (served under John Quincy Adams and Andrew Jackson); 14. James Madison; 15. John Tyler; 16. To preside over the Senate; 17. John Nance Garner; 18. Johnson (three different men); 19. Thomas Jefferson and Richard M. Nixon.

QUIZ 185: WARS _____

1. The War of 1812; 2. Dwight D. Eisenhower; 3. Andrew Jackson; 4. Harry S Truman; 5. William McKinley; 6. Lyndon B. Johnson and Richard M. Nixon (Presidents Dwight D. Eisenhower and John F. Kennedy both sent advisors); 7. Zachary Taylor; 8. Chile; 9. Thomas Jef-

ferson; 10. Theodore Roosevelt; 11. Harry S Truman; 12. Andrew Jackson; 13. Abraham Lincoln; 14. The Civil War; 15. Dwight D. Eisenhower, John F. Kennedy, Lyndon B. Johnson, Richard M. Nixon, and Gerald Ford; 16. World War I; 17. Zachary Taylor; 18. World War I; 19. The War of 1812; 20. Franklin D. Roosevelt.

QUIZ 186: WEAPONS

1. Ronald Reagan; 2. His and Hers; 3. Harry S Truman; 4. James A. Garfield; 5. Martin Van Buren; Extra: Lee Harvey Oswald. Extra: John Wilkes Booth.

QUIZ 187: WEDDINGS

1. Theodore Roosevelt, when Eleanor Roosevelt married Franklin D. Roosevelt; 2. Grover Cleveland; 3. John Tyler; 4. William Holden; 5. John Quincy Adams (his son John Adams married Mary Catherine Hellen); 6. Patricia Nixon and Edward Finch Cox; 7. John Tyler; 8. John Adams, John Quincy Adams, Harry S Truman, and Dwight D. Eisenhower; 9. Nine; 10. Woodrow Wilson.

QUIZ 188: WHITE HOUSE

1. John Adams; 2. To commemorate George Washington's birthday; 3. William H. Harrison and Zachary Taylor; 4. Rutherford B. Hayes; 5. Chester A. Arthur; 6. Theodore Roosevelt; 7. Martha Washington; 8. *Casablanca* (which means White House); 9. Grover Cleveland (and he did return as the twenty-fourth President); 10. Harry S Truman.

QUIZ 189: WITNESSES

1. Edith Roosevelt; 2. John Wilkes Booth; 3. Edith Roosevelt; 4. Harry S and Bess Truman; 5. John Quincy Adams.

QUIZ 190: WORDS AND PHRASES

1. Theodore Roosevelt; 2. Elbridge Gerry; 3. "You lose"; 4. Herbert Hoover; 5. Theodore Roosevelt; 6. John F. Kennedy; 7. Warren G.

Harding; 8. Abraham Lincoln; 9. Martin Van Buren ("Old Kinderhook");
10. Franklin D. Roosevelt; 11. Joel Roberts Poinsett, minister to Mexico
under John Quincy Adams; 12. Rutherford B. Hayes; 13. Alben Barkley;
14. Andrew Jackson; 15. Theodore Roosevelt; 16. "Hooverize"; 17.
Abraham Lincoln; 18. William McKinley; 19. Adlai E. Stevenson; 20.
Spiro T. Agnew.

QUIZ 190: WORLD LEADERS _____

1. The Pope; 2. Herbert Hoover (March 18, 1938); 3. In Teheran; 4.
Nikita Khrushchev; 5. Franklin D. Roosevelt; 6. Napoleon; 7. Fidel
Castro; 8. Dwight D. Eisenhower; 9. Margaret Thatcher (on President
Ronald Reagan); 10. Richard M. Nixon.

QUIZ 192: WOUNDED _____

1. Rutherford B. Hayes; 2. James Monroe; 3. Theodore Roosevelt; 4.
James A. Garfield; 5. James Brady; 6. Andrew Jackson; 7. Andrew
Jackson; 8. James Monroe, Rutherford B. Hayes, and John F. Kennedy;
9. Ronald Reagan; 10. Andrew Jackson.

QUIZ 193: WRITING _____

1. George Washington; 2. James Madison; 3. John Adams; 4. Warren G.
Harding; 5. George Washington and Abraham Lincoln; 6. Calvin
Coolidge; 7. John Quincy Adams; 8. James A. Garfield; 9. Theodore
Roosevelt; 10. Franklin D. Roosevelt.

QUIZ 194: EXTRA #1 _____

1. Eleanor Roosevelt; 2. The key to the Bastille; 3. John F. Kennedy
(fifty-cent piece); 4. Richard M. Nixon (and Gerald Ford); 5. Garret
Hobart.

QUIZ 195: EXTRA #2 _____

1. Thomas Marshall; 2. Richard M. Nixon; 3. *Patton;* 4. Harry S
Truman; 5. Ulysses S. Grant (born Hiram Ulysses Grant).

QUIZ 196: EXTRA #3 ⸻

1. Herbert Hoover; 2. William Henry Harrison; 3. Dolley Madison; 4. Rachel Jackson; 5. Abraham Lincoln.

QUIZ 197: EXTRA #4 ⸻

1. James Knox Polk; 2. Agriculture; 3. James Monroe; 4. George Washington, Zachary Taylor, and Dwight D. Eisenhower; 5. Woodrow Wilson.

QUIZ 198: EXTRA #5 ⸻

1. Xavier Cugat; 2. Woodrow Wilson; 3. Alben Barkley; 4. George Clinton (served under Thomas Jefferson and James Madison) and John C. Calhoun (served under John Quincy Adams and Andrew Jackson); 5. Ulysses S. Grant.

QUIZ 199: EXTRA #6 ⸻

1. Calvin Coolidge; 2. Benjamin Harrison and William Howard Taft; 3. There wasn't any limit; 4. Rachel Jackson; 5. John Quincy Adams.

QUIZ 200: TOUCH AND TRICKY QUESTIONS—THE FINAL TEST ⸻

1. Yes, he had previously seen it in its entirety before seeing it again (in part) on April 14, 1985, the night he was shot; 2. He didn't, it was published in Philadelphia on September 19, 1796; 3. The eighteenth (the nineteenth century began on January 1, 1801); 4. Ulysses S. Grant and Julia Denton Grant; 5. Robert J. Donovan; 6. William Howard Taft (he did accept on the third offer); 7. Edward "Teddy" Kennedy; 8. Norman Thomas, of the Socialist Party (the newspaper was owned by President Warren G. Harding); 9. John Quincy Adams (his brother, Thomas Adams, was the Chief Justice of the Massachusetts State Supreme Court); 10. Yes, of the Fidelity and Deposit Company from 1920 to 1928; 11. William McKinley (he lived in Poland, Ohio); 12. Three (he can hold two full terms, and a partial term if he succeeds to the Presidency with less

than two years left to serve); 13. Alexander Haig, who was representing President Ronald Reagan; 14. John Quincy Adams (but he declined to serve); 15. None (although he graduated from West Point, they weren't giving degrees at the time); 16. Outdoors, although it rained; 17. PT-59 (this was his next assignment after the sinking of his PT-109); 18. George Washington never lived in the White House, but his wife, Martha, lived on her family's Virginia plantation called the White House. 19. Harriet Lane (as the niece of bachelor President James Buchanan, she acted as mistress of the White House).